PRAISE FOR *FALLING FREE*

"Be prepared to have your atrophied, tired notion of God propelled into a new and spacious place. With humor, grace, and not a little jostling of your comfort zone, Shannan Martin will introduce you to the mess at the margins. 'See Jesus in the lowly place,' St. Ignatius writes. You will see Him, in this book, as never before. We are invited here to stare at our 'shared ruin,' so that we can walk away, astounded that we belong to each other."

—GREGORY BOYLE, FOUNDER OF HOMEBOY INDUSTRIES; AUTHOR
OF *TATTOOS ON THE HEART: THE POWER OF BOUNDLESS COMPASSION*

"I love this book! My wish is for us all to live as passionately, humbly, and lovingly as the Martins do!"

—BOB GOFF, *NEW YORK TIMES* BESTSELLING AUTHOR OF *LOVE DOES*

"Engaging, funny, and convicting. Shannan and her family woke up from the American Dream to find the upside-down reality of God better and more beautiful than anything they'd known before. This book shook up my soul and invited me into the adventure of taking Jesus at his word."

—ELLIE HOLCOMB, SINGER-SONGWRITER

"Shannan Martin takes what is regular, ordinary, and small about our story and carries it through the lens of God's invisible kingdom, reminding us that the more we often long for might actually be found in less. She can turn a phrase into something so surprising, so stunning, it will both catch your breath and break your heart. Shannan Martin is one of my favorite writers and *Falling Free* is an exquisite work."

—EMILY P. FREEMAN, AUTHOR OF *SIMPLY TUESDAY:
SMALL-MOMENT LIVING IN A FAST-MOVING WORLD*

"Shannan Martin is quickly becoming one of my favorite people. Not just because of what she writes but because of who she is. That said, *Falling Free* is not only convicting and challenging, it's a refreshing look into her story where we will no doubt find a piece of our own story. It's a book that will lead you to encouragement and freedom by following God whenever to the wherever."

—BRANDON HATMAKER, AUTHOR OF *A MILE WIDE* AND *BAREFOOT CHURCH*

"Read this book, if you dare. Through beautiful prose and glorious storytelling, Shannan has laid out the gospel for us. You cannot read this and walk away as if nothing happened. The Spirit of God is crackling with transformative power in these pages. Open this book. It will open your heart and unlock the wonderful mystery of living the gospel in all of its upside down-ness."

—DEIDRA RIGGS, SPEAKER AND AUTHOR OF *ONE: UNITY IN A DIVIDED WORLD*

"Shannan is a rare and beautiful soul. The way she has moved through pain without bitterness, and lives with deep joy is an inspiration. *Falling Free* is her honest story—and it shows us that trust can be terrifying, hope can hurt, and love can set you free."

—DR. JOHN SOWERS, AUTHOR OF *THE HEROIC PATH*

"*Falling Free* answers the question we all have when we sense God is asking us to give up our dreams: 'Will I be okay?' The answer is a resounding 'YES!' In fact, we'll be freer and more fulfilled. Through Shannan's open and funny writing, I feel like I understand what true freedom in Christ looks like: it's following him with our whole hearts and joining him in his mission to make the world whole—way better than a farmhouse sink and shiplap."

—OSHETA MOORE, SPEAKER, BLOGGER, AND HOST OF THE *SHALOM IN THE CITY* PODCAST

"Shannan Martin is the best friend we all hope for: funny and comforting when the chips are down, but a straight-talker who can also pinpoint the exact hard thing we need to hear. The thing about our version of freedom is that we never fully have it, and Shannan is here to guide us as we learn to give up on our quest to be 'good enough, middle-class enough, or faithful enough.' Her gorgeous words both challenged me to my core and made me float with happiness at all the ways God uses chaotic, messed-up people like myself to bring his kingdom. She is my new favorite theologian, and my new favorite best friend."

—D. L. Mayfield, author of *Assimilate or Go Home: Notes from a Failed Missionary on Rediscovering Faith*

"Reading *Falling Free* is like having a dear friend knock the rose-colored glasses from your face only to replace them with a true, crisp vision—something about freedom that is far more beautiful and surprising, terrible and healing than you could imagine. This isn't the way of a better quiet time or tidier thinking. *Falling Free* is the rip-roarious story of Jesus in the life of Shannan Martin. It's the ravenous, impossible love of God that heals, unhinges, goes for broke, cobbles together, and leads home."

—Amber C. Haines, author of *Wild in the Hollow*

"Shannan, through the words in these pages and in the way she lives out her life, pushes me to betterment. The best thing? She never heaps on the guilt in the process. She just lives her life and tells her story beautifully, and in doing so, she calls us all out of our comfort zones and asks us to examine our choices: *Am I living to be comfortable? Or am I willing to make a difference in an ordinary but important way?* I'm so grateful for her words."

—Tsh Oxenreider, author of *At Home in the World* and *Notes from a Blue Bike*

FALLING
FREE

FALLING
FREE

Rescued from the Life I Always Wanted

SHANNAN MARTIN

NELSON
BOOKS

An Imprint of Thomas Nelson

Published in Nashville, Tennessee, by Nelson Books, an imprint of Thomas Nelson. Nelson Books and Thomas Nelson are registered trademarks of HarperCollins Christian Publishing, Inc.

Published in association with the literary agency of Wolgemuth & Associates, Inc.

Thomas Nelson titles may be purchased in bulk for educational, business, fundraising, or sales promotional use. For information, please e-mail SpecialMarkets@ ThomasNelson.com.

In rare instances, a name has been changed to protect the privacy of the person described. Events and conversations have been constructed from the author's memory.

Unless otherwise noted, Scripture quotations are taken from the *Holy Bible*, New Living Translation. © 1996, 2004, 2007, 2013 by Tyndale House Foundation. Used by permission of Tyndale House Publishers, Inc., Carol Stream, Illinois 60188. All rights reserved.

Scripture quotations marked NIV are from the Holy Bible, New International Version®, NIV®. Copyright © 1973, 1978, 1984, 2011 by Biblica, Inc.® Used by permission of Zondervan. All rights reserved worldwide. www.zondervan.com. The "NIV" and "New International Version" are trademarks registered in the United States Patent and Trademark Office by Biblica, Inc.®

Scripture quotations marked THE MESSAGE are from *The Message*. Copyright © by Eugene H. Peterson 1993, 1994, 1995, 1996, 2000, 2001, 2002. Used by permission of Tyndale House Publishers, Inc.

Library of Congress Cataloging-in-Publication Data

Names: Martin, Shannan, 1976- author.
Title: Falling free : rescued from the life I always wanted / Shannan Martin.
Description: Nashville : Thomas Nelson, 2016.
Identifiers: LCCN 2016004537 | ISBN 9780718077464
Subjects: LCSH: Christian life.
Classification: LCC BV4501.3 .M27635 2016 | DDC 248.4--dc23 LC record available at https://lccn.loc.gov/2016004537

Printed in the United States of America

16 17 18 19 20 RRD 6 5 4 3 2 1

For Cory.
Let's never stop falling together.

CONTENTS

Yet I am confident I will see the LORD's goodness
while I am here in the land of the living.

—PSALM 27:13

FOREWORD

Jen Hatmaker

OKAY FINE. I'LL be honest: Shannan and I first bonded over brine. While I want you to know that we are both women of substance, authenticity requires that confession. We also love pickles. Really, all pickled products. We have had meaningful, passionate conversations about beets. We feel equally devoted to vinegars. We are twin sisters in flavor profiles, and should Cory and Brandon pass away tragically on the same day, we could happily coexist as sister wives, as our youngest daughters are basically the same person and we know how to parent her/them.

I tell you this because I want you to know that Shannan is a trustworthy guide through the conversations in this book. Super uncomplicated, easy stuff like consumerism and poverty and opening your home to incarcerated young adults and selling dream homes. She is you. She is me. She isn't some impossibly precious, otherworldly, international missionary who can't relate to you. Her story feels at once familiar and spectacular, ordinary and exceptional. You will discover that at the same time her words make you squirm, you wish you lived next door to her. You will want her wisdom and you will want her pickles.

These are my favorite types of guides. The ones who say super honest things about feelings and dreams and hang-ups and failures. The ones that don't prescribe a kingdom-centered life without also disclosing their own stumbles and white-knuckled fear along the way. This sort of transparency invites us in, paves a road in our own imaginations, gently shines a light on a road less taken.

And this book holds the story of a road less taken. It will stress you out and give you hope. It will draw you in and freak you out. It will help you take a good, honest look at what you have, where you are, what you want, where you want to go, what you are willing to say yes to, what you are willing to say no to. They are good questions, reader, ones we should be asking and answering.

Shannan never prescribes the answers, by the way. This isn't a life template. It doesn't offer a formula. It is just one person's story. But the underlying currents, the simmering tension, the beautiful kingdom God has invited us all into remain consistent. You will absolutely connect to feelings, Scriptures, longings, frustrations, fears. You will positively identify with expectations, confusion, new vision, neighborliness, surrender. I certainly did.

This was my favorite paragraph in the entire book: "He invites us also into his curious existence and offers to lighten our load so we can finally touch freedom. We'll know it when we see it. Our hearts were created to track it down. He points us toward home, and though we may know little else, we know it's where we belong."

That's the end game for *Falling Free*: freedom. If that is the only promise that draws you in, let me be the first to tell you: you will find it within these pages. To be fair, it may not look one hot iota like what you expected, but you will uncover it nonetheless. Some of the particulars will be unique to Shannan's story, but you will find a hundred points of connection, of recognition, of conviction, and when I think of what God will do with this brave telling in the lives of countless readers, well, I am standing on my tiptoes, watching with bated breath, thrilled to see God's kingdom come in our generation full of ordinary, regular folks prepared to say simply, without fanfare or any sort of savior complex or agenda:

Here we are, God. Send us.

INTRODUCTION

I'M SUPPOSED TO be a farm girl.

Right now I should be wearing a prairie skirt, traipsing barefoot to my gardens, staking my delphinium with vintage ribbon, catching raspberries in the bowl of my apron.

That's how I always saw myself. It was my secret dream, and I knew if I ever got there, I would have made it.

I don't know how I came to this conclusion, or even why. But all my life, people around me referred to acreage, forestland, and crusty barns breathing hay dust through their planks as "God's country." Though I never stopped to think about what that made the rest of the world—or even the rest of my tiny hometown, with its lone flashing traffic light and the fifty-cent pop machine—naming something as "God's" will have an effect on a girl who was taught to love and serve him.

Calling something "God's" will make her want it.

That pretty ideal became my holy grail.

When I married a boy who bought my engagement ring with the seven hundred dollars he'd earned selling his 4-H pig at auction, it was just one more link in the chain. We eventually bought our six acres with a barn creaky enough to warrant caution tape. We planted our gardens and an orchard, and I staked the delphinium only to do it over again for the next three years.

Of course we had made it. We'd secured that romanticized, modern-day *Little House on the Prairie* ideal.

You should have seen the approving nods we received from all God's people.

Tucked in at the end of a longish lane, we got to work raising our family and growing our own herbs.

We didn't come close to being legit, salt-of-the-earth, natural-living homesteaders. We didn't even recycle, but if you repeat that, I will deny it.

What we were was a cute little family living a sweet little life. We mingled among our own, cherished our children, wrote out tithe checks, and beefed up our savings accounts. We contemplated chickens, baked cobblers, and did crafts on the kitchen table.

For four years we wore the quiet country life like our very identity. We buttoned it up and looped it around our necks. We twirled in its pastures, and everything was alive with the sound of croaking frogs and wind blowing across the bean fields. Somewhere along the way, I started a blog and branded myself Flower Patch Farmgirl, building an online community of folks interested in the particular way I played at being a farm girl.

But sometimes, when the sun sank down to the edges of our world, Cory and I wondered why God didn't feel nearer now that we shared an address. We never asked the question out loud. We didn't dare admit our doubts.

And then, before we knew it, it was all gone.

In ways that seemed both dramatic and snail-paced, God got

our attention and called our family out and away. He scrubbed away our distractions and plainly showed us how we'd gotten it so wrong for so long. Our life was in direct contradiction to the one we'd been charged to live, not because it was bad—I'll never stop trying to perfect the humble peach cobbler, and a life without a garden is one I'd rather not endure—but because it was fundamentally about *us*. Our focus was locked on ourselves. Our security. Our future.

Our plans.

For all the years we spent reading about loving our neighbors and massaging the words to fit our comfy existence, for all the ways we tried to hold on to the life we thought we wanted, assuring ourselves it was God's will, in no time flat we were upturned, dangling by our ankles, positioned in such a way that the world would never again look right unless it was upside-down, inside-out, or, at the very least, bent badly to one side.

Right now, outside my window, grimy snow coats the curbs while my neighbor's flag from the Fourth of July flaps in the breeze like a hand against a heart. *This is my country now, and my allegiance is here.*

Our kids, while impossibly cute—sharing not an ounce of my big-eared DNA, hallelujah—play and gripe down the hall. Our oldest, newest son stands on the front stoop with a cigarette at his lips and a plastic Community Corrections tracking bracelet locked around his ankle. A few miles away, my chaplain husband makes his way home from the county jail.

The world outside our windows is a mash-up of buckled sidewalks, heartbroken humans, truant teenagers, and the occasional peal of mariachi. *This* is God's country. We fit right in.

This city, this life, it owns us now. I'm sure we had a choice along the way, but saying no seemed so much riskier than saying yes.

Christians like to say God can use us wherever we are, and it's true. But sometimes we hide in that truth. We wiggle our shoulders down into wherever it is we happen to be—the place we prefer to remain, thank you very much—until all we can see are the things we want to see and "being used by God" becomes little more than waving to the neighbor across the way or teaching our children that lying is always a sin, no matter what.

Noble feats, yes, and not necessarily even small.

But they're starting points, not destinations.

In order to find real freedom, we have to be willing to fall into the arms of our Savior, who knows a thing or two about low places.

The Jesus I love walked the earth in muddy shoes. He was a free-range Savior, a homeless healer, sent to earth to show us how to live if heaven really is our prize.

These days I picture Jesus in faded jeans and a rocker T. Maybe a flannel when it's cold. I mean, the robe he wears in most pictures is fine. That image served me well for more than thirty years. But Jesus is as relevant here in my new neighborhood as he was in ancient Samaria. The Jesus who dismantled the life I chose didn't call my name from centuries ago or from foreign lands. He descended from heaven and donned a belted toga for John and Rahab and Zacchaeus, and he does the same for us, meeting us right in this moment, wholly with us in our messed-up world.

God met my family in our unassuming life and, with all the love he's made of, showed us that the keys to his kingdom are only ours when we surrender the flimsy, stage-set kingdoms built with our own savvy and style.

Rending us from all we thought we were, he dropped us smack-dab in the middle of everything we'd spent a lifetime avoiding, with our palms facing up.

All we had was his.

God gives. He takes away.

His glory could mean castles, but not for me.

His glory is secondhand sandals caked in grime. His glory is good gifts that often look small and messy and a head-scratcher economy where we lack nothing as long as we surrender everything.

God rescued me from the life I always wanted. He plucked my family up from our dream farmhouse, stripped us of our financial stability and personal esteem, and shattered our obsessions with security, safety, and common sense.

Without warning he yanked the rungs from the ladder we were busy climbing, and we fell. Down at his feet, unburdened of the things we'd held so tightly in our desperate quest for freedom, we found the life we were made for. The answer wasn't in our shipshape self-sufficiency or see-what-I-can-do efforts. It wasn't in the muscle and drive it takes to get ourselves to the top. Rather, it was in the weightless free fall to the bottom, where he handed us his very best gifts—an income on life support, a zip code on the wrong side of the tracks, a new son with a criminal record, and friends hungry for food, Jesus, and nicotine. We had no choice but to trust God to help us stick the landing. The freedom was in the falling.

1

GET RISKY

When we risk our lives to run after Christ, we discover the safety that is found only in his sovereignty, the security that is found only in his love, and the satisfaction that is found only in his presence.

—RADICAL, DAVID PLATT[1]

A FEW MILES across town stands a church with one of those big signs that showcases inspiring or condemning blurbs via clipped-on plastic letters. In regular rotation is the ominous "God is always watching," and though it might be intended in a "You're never alone!" sentiment, I always read it with a rumble of dread, glancing over my shoulder and warily checking the sky. I assume these blanket statements, entirely divorced from all context, do not compel sinners through the church doors, much less to the saving grace of Jesus. I'm confident we can do better than this, but it's only the first paragraph of my story, and already I digress.

A perkier line in the church's message rotation is, "God is all we need!"

I can't argue with this one, but I sure want to.

The bare-naked reality is that I haven't experienced a single moment in my life where all I had was God. I came close, though, the night a few years back when I was alone in my hotel room in Addis Ababa, Ethiopia. I was part of a group of influencers doing PR for Mocha Club[2] and fashionABLE,[3] two gutsy, forward-thinking nonprofit groups that work to fight poverty throughout twelve countries in Africa. My team had been carefully curated to include impossibly cool and savvy women whose effortless style was in no way dulled by third-world surroundings. Aside from my travel mates' exceptional kindness and unflappable fashion sense, several were also legitimately famous.

Meanwhile I had packed for comfort and didn't own a smartphone.

The day before, when one of them asked to see a picture of my family, I had pulled actual paper snapshots from my wallet and passed them around the table to the sound of polite crickets. Never had I been so certain about the full scope of my social inadequacies. I felt ill, and I didn't yet know that actual vomiting was closing in on my horizon.

That night as I sat in my hotel room, separated by entire continents from the comfort of my home and my people, I was green at the gills and feeling like the only high schooler still wearing a training bra.

Everything in me wanted to run to my husband, Cory, or to the solace of my parents. Heck, the persistently friendly produce guy from Kroger would have been useful in the pinch I was in. I needed a real person, someone with skin, who knew things about me and loved me anyway, or at the very least remembered how I prefer my watermelons. Any one of them would have helped. But time zones worked against me, and I found myself entirely alone in the throes of a personal minibreakdown.

My only plan for survival was to endure the night by escaping into sleep, just as I had endured countless family road trips throughout my adolescence. Though my strategy may have worked with a fifteen-hour, midwinter trip back in 1992, on this night it proved wholly impossible.

Somewhere between the hours of 3:00 and 4:00 a.m., it struck me that God was all I had, and he would have to be enough, just as he'd always promised. (That it took me so long to acknowledge this truth speaks to my spiritual condition in a way that we simply do not have time to explore.)

And he was. God was totally enough. He got me through that night, but the hard truth is, he wasn't truly *all* I had. For one thing, my night of transcontinental angst was spent hunkered down in a beautiful hotel set against the backdrop of a country chewed up by a history of poverty and victimization. I swallowed down meds with clean bottled water while surfing the web from a laptop computer that had traversed the globe in a special case meant to ensure its safe transport. In terms of personal catastrophe, I was doing all right, and that was before I remembered I had God too.

In a world where we possess the power to distract or buy our way out of most discomfort, can we ever really mean it when we say God is all we need? Can untested words ring anything but hollow from our lips?

Faithful and capable folk, we parrot familiar phrases from a place of theory rather than practice and warm ourselves by their feel-good, holy glow. But please don't press us. We don't really know if we actually believe them. No matter what happens, no matter what hard thing we face or how we run to God at the very end after we've exhausted all other options, no matter how misunderstood or hurt or even physically ill we may be, we hold plenty of self-concocted painkillers to buffer us from the ravages of real-world living.

There are the obvious safety nets, like heated homes, city water, and the FDA. But what about stable, prolific employment opportunities? Houses of worship we attend without risk to our lives? Then there are the dead bolts and password-protected financial accounts. Speaking of which, how often do we apply our credit lines like a salve to our wounds?

We have relentless updates on the proper positioning of our newborns in their cribs and three-point harnessed car seats for our toddlers. We have EpiPens, expiration dates, full-coverage insurance, low-VOC paint, and 401(k)s. There are color-coded systems for pollen counts, UV rays, and air travel. We have helmets and knee pads, accountants and pastors, and tiny bottles of Thieves essential oils knocking around in our seasonal purses.

There are other things, too, like communities where we blend in perfectly, churches where we won't ever feel uncomfortable, schools where our children are promised an excellent (and free) education, and neighbors we don't actually know, yet trust all the same, primarily because they remind us of ourselves.

We stand in worship services and sing our hearts out about things like faith and trusting God in deep waters. We say God is all we need, but what we really mean is, "All we need is God, our family, the promise of safety, and money." We roll everything into a ball. We smoosh it together. Our money and our family came from God, right? So it's fine. They're essentially one and the same.

We sing like we mean it while we pray to God we'll never find out if we really do.

What would happen if everything but God were swept away? Would he really be enough? I'm confident I'll never find out, and I'm honest enough to admit that I hope I won't.

But I can tell you from experience that when just a small part of my world was swept away, it rocked me so hard my teeth rattled for months. It was utterly discombobulating. I had wound God so tightly with my externals, I wasn't sure how to separate the two. I didn't recognize this God who asked to be enough in the face of substantial financial loss and the mere thought of danger. This wasn't the God I wanted to need.

Like that night in the Ethiopian hotel, when God's voice got louder in my ear about the places he'd like me to go and the stuff he'd like me to surrender, I simply did not know how to deal. He was asking difficult things of my family, specifically, to sell the home we'd worked so hard for and to move into the unknown. He was pulling us from shore. The earliest days of wrestling God for what I desperately wanted to keep organized themselves into a muddy processional of pain and confusion, an acute sensation of loss and longing, and emotional cloud cover. I knew I was being a wimp, overreacting and hyperdramatizing. But the terrain was foreign and rocky, and I was way out of shape.

Leaving Eden

The first time I drove down the street where we now live, it was raining, the chilly drizzle that can feel a bit like hamstrung

5

hope. My youngest, Silas, sat unusually quiet in his car seat in what could have either been a blessing or an omen. We crept uphill past the ruins of other lives: crumbling bricks; drab, faded siding; cracked windowpanes; and splitting porch rails. Three hundred feet of mostly brokenness and decay.

It was an unlikely mini-adventure fueled by no more than a hunch. Squeezed into the two-hour time slot of our daughter Ruby's preschool class, we headed to check out the city where we thought God might be leading our family.

As stubborn as I am about being right, I was hoping we'd gotten this one wrong.

My heart pounded as I dialed the radio down to a hush. I knew leaving our home in the country would be painful. My white-knuckled attachment to my easy, wannabe farm girl existence was what had gotten me into this mess in the first place. The truth had descended on me like an early fog—it's hard to pine for heaven when you already believe you're there.

Still, I wasn't sure I could live in this neighborhood. In fact, I was almost positive I couldn't. There were gangs in this city, I'd heard. There was crime. Drugs. From his front porch, a hawkish neighbor watched me between long drags on his cigarette, telling me everything I needed to know. This was the kind of place you resign yourself to, a place you find yourself stuck. It was certainly not a place you choose. That's what I thought back then.

I drove north, mental images of my friendless children and my shy, scaredy-cat self burning my eyes. We would never fit in here. Our lives had done exactly nothing to prepare us for this reality.

"This could be our home," I told Silas, the syllables and spaces in between my words catching in my throat as I tried on what I hoped wouldn't fit. While the neighborhood wasn't an inner-city slum, my dad would never describe it as "God's country." Safety and security, the twin pillars of a good, Christian life, lost their meaning in this urban unknown. I was way out of my element. An imposter.

With every desperate roofline and every sagging porch, dread lodged deeper in my chest. A left turn, then another, we came to a stop behind two new homes. Though not ball gowns by any stretch, they were solid business casual in a jungle of grease-stained jeans. We'd been told there were plans for three more, after the existing abandoned homes lining the block were carted off, brick by brick.

The yards were small, with slopes that eluded common sense. There was maybe enough level ground for a small swing set. Maybe.

My eyes fell on Silas in the rearview mirror, and a fresh wave of panic pulled me under. Our kids were giving up six acres, a giant swing set, a trampoline, and enough bike-riding perimeter to make them good and sweaty. The least they deserved was a decent yard.

I bawled my eyes out.

Then I drove away.

I drove back through town, past the familiar places where we shopped and ate. I drove down quiet, tree-lined roads. I wept and I drove without slowing until we were tucked safely in our six-bedroom home down the longish lane. *This* place was our dream, and we finally held it with both hands. It was part of us, and we carried it in our hearts like life's ultimate, grown-up lovey—a security blanket of sorts. How could we ever lay it down? What was the point in finally landing *here* just to end up *there*? How could we not have a little less of God if we abandoned his country?

But God had pulled back just enough of the curtain to make our hearts beat faster. It was compelling. It was bananas. At our core, we were still Cory and Shannan, entirely human and glaringly ill equipped for change. Who were we to believe we were being called to city living? I had no frame of reference for jam-packed community or even next-door neighbors. My childhood had centered on trips to the village library, the woods across the road, and church. If pressed, I'm going to say the woods prepared me more for urban living than church ever did, but only because my friend Angie and I once tried to plant a garden in a weed-riddled patch of its dry, shaded earth. We did every single thing wrong, but a lone carrot still grew.

This calling felt preposterous, as if we were two kids playing pretend. I was a college graduate before I felt confident traversing a crosswalk, for the love of Pete.

For all of our adult lives, our radar had been locked on one goal: to ensure our own safety and security. We were hardwired to focus on solving our own problems and applauded by the church when we constructed a life that pointed directly at the American Dream, with a side of Jesus.

This calling, this threat to our personal security, was nothing short of monumental. We were moving into level-red territory. Everything seemed foreign, so we did what most humans do in the midst of uncertainty—we conjured some broad, bleak assumptions about the unknown, chief of which was the naive, oppressive belief that people different from us were inherently, primarily dangerous; perhaps not individually, but certainly in the crammed-in, close-city quarters collective.

At the same time we started to wonder what we might be missing. We were cautiously intrigued. Back at the farm we were getting a little desperate to experience some of the mess of the gospel, the parts that come with rowdy redemption and wide-eyed trust, and even the parts that promise pain and land good folks in the same trenches where Jesus chose to spend his time. We wanted to feel something beyond ourselves. We wanted to be free.

Sometimes gently, other times bossy as all get-out, God pointed to that forgotten neighborhood at the fringes of the city. His people needed neighbors, and we could do that. He promised we could. We could simply go, as though he meant it each of the hundreds of times he says throughout the Bible to go, as in literally, move your feet, guys.

Without much fanfare, after a string of teary nights, we took that next little leap. We put the farm on the market. I plucked my lifelong dream of country living like a tick from my heart and tossed it onto the fire without an inkling of how much brighter that altar would burn.

This was the step that took us public. The plans brewing quietly in our hearts were now stitched to our sleeves.

Almost no one understood. People were concerned and skeptical. They stared at us with their heads cocked to the side. They told us this was our Isaac, a test from God to see if we would be obedient. "Congratulations!" they said. "You passed!"

The overwhelming message we received was that God didn't actually want us to do this upside-down thing of abandoning more for less. We were getting it all wrong. He simply wanted us to prove our loyalty by being willing.

Friends spoke to us gently, with strained worry. For the most part, they thought we were straight nuts.

On the one hand, I totally related. Up to that precise moment, I would have thought the same. On the other hand, if we were hearing from God, it didn't matter how countercultural it seemed to everyone else.

Longing to make sense of things in the midst of our reservations, I became obsessed with figuring out who Jesus really is, whether these shocking things we believed we were hearing were consistent with his character and how he spent his time on earth. What did he do? How did he live? What mattered to him?

What we saw with fresh eyes was that God's "more" often looks a whole lot like less. In this upside-down kingdom his best gifts are not found on the tallest shelf at the end of a strenuous climb. They're found in the dirt. They're low and humble, lacking as far as we're concerned. He sends his people to do wild, gutsy, backward things for his glory. His refusal to bend to popular convention is his signature move.

His Son was no exception. God didn't ask Jesus to come to earth just to see if he would be willing. He moved Jesus down to earth, where he would spend his first night as a helpless infant, squirming in a feed trough, sheltered by a stable, in the shabby town of Bethlehem. This wasn't accidental, and God didn't merely allow it to haphazardly happen this way. It had been ordered for all of eternity, with great intention.

As Jesus grew into a man, the pattern continued. Nothing about his life was sequestered or esteemed. He fled from high places and gravitated toward wells and jam-packed homes. He was allergic to stockpiling and actively chose risk and adventure, shaking the status quo from its foundation. Jesus traveled to towns where he had no business being and didn't give a rip what anyone had to say about it. He had no home, no cash, and, I'll assume, no high-end, all-terrain sandals.

In striking contrast we prized a quiet existence marked by comfort, ease, and ironclad safety. We disguised our entitlement by calling it a blessing.

We were far away from the life of Jesus. We weren't even across-town neighbors.

This revelation spelled real trouble: thumping-hearts, crying-in-the-shower, how-did-we-miss-this turmoil in the third degree.

It's worth noting that I grew up in full-immersion Evangelicalism. I sort of thought I knew it all. I had memorized the code. I bought the shirt—and I unfortunately mean this in a literal way, as my high school wardrobe-of-choice included a rotation of men's XL T-shirts emblazoned with various obscure religious messages that only other Christians could decode. I had all the trappings but didn't grasp the why of the life I had chosen. I toed the line. I did what I was told. I was a total good girl (except for when I wasn't, which, by the way, I would rather not talk about).

I sometimes envy people who found God later in the game. It used to be because their stories were richer and more exciting. They could light up a testimony hour with just one strike of their world-weary battle tales. They were the closers, saved until the very end of the service, while the rest of us sat pale and infant-skinned against the blaze of their redemption.

I envy them now because their first taste of Christ and his kingdom can be savored by a life that has known his absence, while my first memory of Jesus involves a flannel board and generic Oreos. Not bad things, but lacking in personal impact or spiritual drama. God was always part of my background. I knew no other way. So ingrained were the stories of Moses in his basket, the guys in the fiery furnace, David and all his woes, they blurred against my own edges. I knew them, but I struggled to see their significance in my life. I accepted them as a hazy yet vital part of my history, never stopping to wonder how they were relevant *today*. Assuming, in fact, that they weren't.

With hungry hearts all these years later, however, we began to see exactly why the stories of risk woven throughout Scripture were written precisely for us. There's a kinship among Jesus and his people, and it has something to do with chucking the common sensibilities of the world into the Dumpster. It's got something to do with riding the train clean off the rails and swerving away from all the law-abiding citizens in order to land in the gutter— that place we were never supposed to be. The doubters from our clean-cut, farm-loving life only confirmed that this fresh vision was from God alone, shot straight to our hearts. It was a beautiful thing.

We bought one of those new houses on the drab side of town and counted the days until it would be ready, not necessarily sure what we were supposed to do in our new neighborhood once we got there.

As the time drew closer, we found ourselves over there often, checking the progress and feeling our way around our new digs. The niggling fear of the unknown was receding.

And then we visited the park.

For all the brutality of a northern Indiana winter, come mid-July, the sun wilts us just as it does everyone else. The neighborhood park, positioned a stone's throw from our future front door, was hopping. A month away from our move, I was eager to try our new surroundings on for size. My three young kiddos in tow, we trucked across the street while Cory hung back, painting planks for our living room walls.

It was pure chaos, and not just the usual kind where kids run screaming through sprinklers, racing and shouting and whooping it up. There was another kind of chaos in the mix, the kind I'd always avoided.

Two young moms sunned themselves at the fringes of the splash pad as though it were Daytona Beach, sporting, let's just say, really tiny bathing suits. They didn't speak to their kids as much as repeatedly scream at them. They barked orders, and when the kids didn't listen, they cussed them clean out, making threats I hoped were empty.

I fought the urge to register visible shock or disgust. I willed myself to remain neutral, to at least pretend I could do this. *We can do this.* Finding her a willing distraction, I struck up a conversation with an adorable blondie in a cockeyed ponytail. She was heading to school in the fall, along with my kids Calvin and Ruby. When I asked her what grade she'd be in, she set her jaw and answered, "That one where they teach you your ABCs." Her eyes locked on mine with the air of someone four times her age. A few minutes later, she flung her tattered bath towel over her shoulder and walked up the street, five years old and totally alone. Her frame receded into the horizon, then disappeared.

These were my neighbors. I was called not to pretend I could save them, but to love them, to simply be with them. They bore the very image of Christ himself. They were needy in ways I had judged, but also in ways that backed me into the corner of "me, too." How many times had I been unfair as a mom, or even shamefully unkind? They may have worn their junk in more obvious ways, but mine was just as ugly. I was simply conditioned to hide it or mold it into something more socially acceptable and middle-class. My life knew support, encouragement, and resources theirs would never touch; yet, just like them, I still spent my days treading the waters of impatience and selfishness, hungry for the wrong kinds of love, longing for a moment of peace somewhere sunny, preferably with a friend at my side.

There existed so much overlap between the two women cooking in the sun and the one watching in judgment from the canopy of the maple tree. I just didn't know it yet.

That night, after the kids were tucked in, the full weight of what we were about to do landed like an "I told you so." My tears fell hot as I wallowed in a place of crushing worry.

I thought we should bail. Everyone was right; we would ruin our kids. This wasn't God speaking; this was thrill-seeking or gunning for a sparklier crown. Our motives were all wrong. We would never fit in. We'd regret this for the rest of our lives at best, lose our very selves at worst.

I sobbed into my pillow, thinking about Calvin, Ruby, and Silas, all fast asleep in our safe, little home in a town where everyone, for the most part, looked and lived the same. Would my kids have friends in the city? Could I trust my neighbors with them? Was the guy at the hardware store right—would Calvin join a gang? Would Silas buy drugs? Would terror prowl around Ruby like an unchained dog?

Those seeds of doubt tossed out by concerned, loving people found fresh soil in my mama's heart. When night screams down the track like pitch-dark dread, yes, it's possible to imagine a preschooler with a drug habit. Fear defies common sense. It takes shape out of nothing, then barges in and fills the room.

For more than a year we had dodged the skeptics, including the hairdresser, the convenience store clerk, and a host of well-meaning friends who wondered why on earth we would move from our tightly knit, quaint community into this one, which had seemingly morphed into a wolves' den. Staring up at the ceiling through my tears, I swore I heard howling.

I'd always been taught that a lack of peace meant God was sending an "abort mission" smoke signal. It's among the most beloved excuses in the church-culture canon. We toss it out, and no one can argue. "I don't have peace about it." Boom. End of discussion.

What I was feeling that night wasn't a lack of peace though. It was boring, old fear.

God, in his infinite greatness, could have done whatever it took—anything—to put an end to this would-be fiasco, if it was, in fact, that. He didn't need fear in his arsenal. Though God speaks to us in many ways, he never does so through fear. No. He is love—as in, it doesn't even exist apart from him. As Love, he's the top dog driver-away of fear. Fear incinerates in his light.

With great tenderness my barn-burning God led me, in the midst of my fear, to those still waters I'd read about all my life. He restored my soul as I lay wrecked and weary in my ratty sweats. He reminded me who he is—a God who laughs in the face of logic and weighs things like safety and security on an eternal scale requiring all of my faith. He reminded me about Jesus and how he loves me and my kids completely. Foolishly.

This is the Jesus who beat down my door and screamed my

name. (In love.) This is the one who pointed my eyes past my own horizon to show me the rest of God's kingdom and all the ways it stood ready to fit his will, right here, as it does in heaven.

Jesus painted a clear picture of my stubborn and dishonest refusal to do the job I'd been given—*love your neighbor as much as you love yourself, Shannan*. He spray-painted it across the serene backdrop of the life I'd created, then gave me another chance. It's what he's famous for.

The Unlearning

We so often say we believe that there is no safer place than the center of God's will, but we refuse to believe he would ever lead us to places of brokenness or danger.

Afflicted with relentless humanity, we view the world with person-eyes, then project what we see onto the flawless creator of the universe, assuming he operates as we do. We trick ourselves into thinking God is just a holier version of us—our brain, our worldview, none of the sinfulness. We forget that while we bear his image and harbor all his love, we can't comprehend the scope of eternal reality from our anthill vantage point. We say we trust God's will but feel so much better if we run ahead of him with our dustpan and broom, doing what we can to eliminate pain and minimize risk.

When we gauge our sense of security on things like low crime rates, high-achieving schools, and padded retirement accounts, what we're essentially saying is, "We'll take care of ourselves, thank you very much. We've got this." We're throwing our full support and all our faith behind ourselves and other imperfect humans just like us. We're living life as though God is only as big as we are, that he's basically one of us, that our wisdom is interchangeable.

We keep forgetting who he is and how he loves us.

Faith points to a way that's completely different. It requires us to abandon our lives into the hands of God and whatever he has planned. This is the road that leads to freedom and to fulfilling our mission during our time on earth.

Jesus had a habit of sending people to strange places to do really off-the-wall things. I don't remember how I mentally catalogued this growing up. It's not as if I didn't know. But for some reason, I convinced myself it was irrelevant to me.

As it turns out, just as God called Jesus to courageously buck the system and go to hard places, he bestows on us the same mantle.

In the curious case of the Martin family, this necessitated holding our ideas about security loosely, laying down our pet safety nets, redefining success, and welcoming pain and uncertainty with wide-stretched arms. It meant trading more for less and leaping off the ladder of upward mobility only to hit the dirt and discover we'd had a taste for it all along. It meant making our home among gang members, addicts, and honest families doing their best. More than anything, it meant discovering the golden thread that connects all of us, the glimmering kinship of being fully known in the eyes of another and believing we share a humanity that transcends race, DNA, habits, opportunities, failures, and socioeconomic strata. As we owned up to our failings, we received buckets of grace and gratitude and found more of God in all the places within us that were disappointing and awkward.

It was old pain wrapped in a new beginning, the age-old story of humanity and a promise of redemption. We were on a new road to unlearning what we thought we knew about God in order to really see him at work in and around us.

He wasn't as predictable and safe (or boring) as I secretly believed. He was a quick-darting hummingbird, a solar eclipse, a ripe cherry tomato growing from a raspberry cane. He was a maverick, loud and funny, the best kind of bossy. He was unexpected. Dizzying, even.

And we were worthless outside of his rescue.

Last week I found a picture of myself back on our farm. Staring at it, I could feel the air on my skin and recall with precision the way the clouds used to lean into the horizon, drifting out across our garden and past our distant neighbor's silo. Calvin and Ruby were babies then, and I was too. I remembered the moment we'd stood by the fence and smiled for the camera, but for the life of me I couldn't remember who I was.

I know I had heartaches and fears, but pain had not yet become an inextricable part of me. I didn't think much about global poverty or the way little girls are trafficked and sold. I had two children of minority races, and I still had the gall to believe racism wasn't my problem. I wasn't really aware that there were good people mired in generational poverty and addiction nearby. I thought slumlords and pimps were only in Chicago or New York. We focused on ourselves. Our hearts almost never broke.

That girl only knew the flannel-board Jesus, too two-dimensional to reach into her world and shake it like a jar of nuts. She didn't know him enough to trust him. Her faith was built on things like college degrees and retirement funds. Her life fit lock-and-key with her context.

I'm sure it felt good, aside from the spiritual emptiness. But mercifully that's not where God left her.

Now, every day I am offered the gift of living in such a way that I get a taste of what it means to need him. Resting fully dependent in the palm of his hand, I realize the safety of staying small. I get to embrace the full shock value of the kingdom of God, and that is the real blessing. I get to be knocked around by the fallout of belonging to a life where I am wildly ill equipped to meet its demands. I am honored to experience an existence marked by dependence, where I submit to God's will for my life, even and especially when it defies my put-on, middle-class values.

All the waiting, all the missteps, the wreckage of my defenses, my shattered self-pride, every difficult step along the way brought my family and me to this place where it feels really safe to get a little risky. Who knew?

In this kingdom, where heaven meets earth, God's best hangs sharply off-center. Here, where we receive the gift of partnering with our holy God to reach his people through his love, safety means jumping in the nearest ditch, and reckless is the goal.

2

REDEFINE FAMILY

The problem with the world is that we draw the circle of our family too small.

—Mother Teresa

UP UNTIL MY late twenties, the desire to be a mom was hidden deep inside my sharp angles and dreamy bookishness, boxed up and left waiting on a shelf. I went through the typical baby doll phase as a kid, with my knockoff Cabbage Patch doll in his vaguely nautical sweat suit (hey, Jonathan!), but the sentiment was always more boredom-buster than determined practice. Unlike many of my friends, I didn't want to grow up one day and be a mom. I wanted to be a doctor and a "ceramic lady"—one who casts ceramics, not a fragile tchotchke woman. It marked me in a small and unusual way. Though no one was particularly concerned, people noticed. My older brother told me more than once that I probably shouldn't ever be a mom since I didn't even appreciate our barn cats.

Deep down I knew better. One day I would have kids, maybe even a lot of them. I would do what nearly every woman in my life up to that point had done: get married and have babies. I knew I'd want that one day. I just wasn't sure when.

It turned out the "when" came in our fourth year of marriage, while we were living in an overpriced apartment just outside Washington, DC. I hadn't grown up to be a doctor after all, and I'd never even been near a kiln. Instead, Cory and I were thick in the Capitol Hill rat race, working late and fielding confused looks about why we'd married before we were thirty. We carried our dream for a family like an egg on a spoon, and when the sun sank low through the bank of windows overlooking a parking lot and a Dumpster, I'd stare at the orangey parquet floors and imagine what would come next. Nothing had changed except my heart, yet I felt older, more capable. I was finally, firmly, a member of that elusive club of women who'd always known their purpose was to create life. At last, those dormant cat-fears could be put to rest. I was made to be a mother too. I just took the long way to the conclusion.

I got to work daydreaming about kids made in my own image, or preferably in Cory's. I knew the boys would be fair-skinned, with classically rugged names like John and Joe. The girls would have glossy brown hair. If God was on the throne, no one would inherit my knobby knees or sticking-out ears. And all their eyes would be blue. "The kids" wouldn't be athletically inclined, but they'd laugh easily and crush the annual spelling bee. They'd eat their beets and appreciate the fine art of napping.

I couldn't wait to meet them.

Ditching the pills, we started "trying" with gusto, but the

months stacked on top of each other, and it wasn't long before my master plan felt wobbly. While some women face infertility with deep grief and even depression, I defaulted to annoyance and stubborn resolve. It was tremendously frustrating to meet a problem I couldn't solve with my go-to tools of razor wit, solid critical thinking skills, a propensity to crank out good work in the eleventh hour, and general glass-half-fullness.

Summoning every ounce of knowledge I'd gleaned from my work as a research assistant at, of all places, a think tank, I hit my dial-up Internet with a fierceness I didn't realize was in me. I scoured forums and sniffed out tips and tricks like a modern-day, emotionally volatile, considerably older Nancy Drew. In the name of my would-be brunette firstborn (a girl named Stella, if you're curious), I chugged cough medicine, hoarded ovulation kits, and awkwardly uninvited Cory's friend, whose planned overnight visit fell during, uh, *peak season*.

When none of that worked, we found a quirky specialist and carved a path between our home and his office. At each visit he'd cock his head to the side and stare at me as though I were an obscure riddle. "Why aren't you pregnant yet?" he'd ask. Then he'd prescribe shots, tests, lots of rest, and the odd exploratory surgery.

Eventually enough was enough. Lying there on the exam table, tears running off my face and collecting in the ears I hoped to spare my offspring, I was done. I was done trying, done tempting fate, done praying for something that might never have been meant for me. I was done hoping for the wrong thing, done spending money on a heartache. I was simply, profoundly done.

What I didn't know then is that surrender is always the beginning of a better dream.

Gotcha

Growing up, I knew just a few kids who had been adopted. I heard bits and pieces about their "gotcha days," and the concept always made sense to me. It seemed like a pretty sweet way to remember a significant day-in-the-life, for everyone involved.

The day we met our first son, Calvin, was basically rainbows and sun-showers. It was surreal, dreamy. I paced the floor of the airport terminal while butterflies flapped in my stomach. I scanned every face de-boarding the plane from South Korea, searching for the round-faced four-month-old who would make me a mama. He finally emerged in the arms of his escort, a kind stranger willing to care for him during the bravest leap of his life. The moments that followed were a blur of tears as I locked eyes with my Korean son for the first time. He reached out and clasped his tiny fist around the strand of beads I wore as if grabbing hold of his future. His lips puckered as he searched my unfamiliar face, and I whispered in his tiny ear, "I'm your mommy." This faux-hawked infant with the soul of a wizened retiree leaned in, and I swear he understood.

Without realizing it our hearts were being shifted. We were on our way to a new perspective on orphan care and global causes, but we had to wait for the new-parent dust to settle before we could understand any of it. Our hearts and minds were fixed on the immediacy of the needs in front of us—namely, how would we keep Calvin awake for his last bottle? What was the best way to spend the endless stretch of hours before dinner? And would any of us ever experience REM sleep again?

If you'd asked me that first year whether I believed in celebrating gotcha days, I'm sure I'd have said yes. But that's only because I didn't realize they would get so much harder from there.

The moment I met our precious Ruby, minutes after her birth, she was in the arms of her soulful, warrior birth mom. I stood nearby under a fluorescent glare, the sterility of the delivery room banging against the relief, the pain, the warmth, the tenderness, the compassion, the wanting, the awkwardness, the grace. The love. I struggled to find my place in a moment I couldn't begin to process, one that would indelibly shape the rest of our lives, desperate to somehow dull the pain that ricocheted around the room. If there is no greater joy than meeting the eyes of your child for the first time, there might be no greater ache than watching another woman do the same, then hand her very flesh to you. Our hearts made room for each other as the world spun around, the birth of an unexpected family that would walk untold miles together, bound forever by the palpable nearness of God, who does not turn away from our sadness and shares the richness of our joy.

On Silas's gotcha day, his beloved foster mom crumbled under the weight of her loss while we wobbled on the line between forfeit and gift, retreating to the periphery of pain that wasn't ours and feeling selfish for the ways we wanted it all to play out differently. A cheery yellow sofa juxtaposed the mood of the room as a battery-powered toy airplane piped Korean children's songs into the dense air between us. We watched our son press light-up buttons, breaking into a grin for just a second before remembering his alarm, nervously watching the door again, looking for his mother, not aware that I was already there.

I passed him shrimp-flavored crackers, feigning compo-
sure while warning shots fired inside me. The complexity of the
moment was written across our baby's face, and if I linger too
long on what it felt like to look into his giant almond eyes as his
world was being simultaneously stripped from and handed to
him, well, it takes me a while to recover.

I already loved him enough to wish that I could somehow
spare him from what he didn't yet comprehend. My first hours
as his mama ended with him surrendering to the force of his
heartache, falling asleep, fully spent, in my arms. When he
woke, he remembered, *this is still happening*, and his grief played
on a slow, long loop. He found no solace in our eyes as we held
him on the long flight home, and the days and months (years?)
that followed formed a long processional of his unwavering sorrow. All the while, our love for him grew wilder, crashing into
his confusion and throwing off sparks.

Though we didn't realize it then, adoption was our earliest
entry point away from the comfort of the status quo and through
the doorway of tangible distress and loss. It was here that I
began to see, for the first time, that perhaps what the world calls
"brokenness" can be a thing of real beauty, adorned in the best
possible ways, unexpected and entirely holy.

Though I know many people who adopt with selfless intentions, we were not necessarily among them. We didn't adopt
because God said to care for the orphan. We simply wanted
a family, and we came to see that ours would be built in this
unconventional way. We were happily thrust into the roles of
Mommy and Daddy, remembering only in patches that it wasn't
the norm, and there was sure to be fallout.

● ● ●

Perhaps three of the most frustrating words to an adoptive parent are "your own kids." Unfamiliar with the nuances of adoption lingo, many well-meaning people default to a ledger-sheet mentality of family. There are the children you adopted, and most people are quick to congratulate and coo, but way over on the other side are "your own kids." "Do you think you'll ever have your own kids?" "Were you unable to have your own kids?"

Calvin, Ruby, and Silas were immediately and emphatically ours. They belonged to us in ways that flipped our old, linear definition of "family" end over end. There's something about being handed a precious, treasured child by his or her lion-hearted birth parent that sears every upside-down truth into our souls. These kids are never only "ours." Not in the way we'd like to think. They're on loan to us by a God who is a "Father to the fatherless" (Ps. 68:5), one who never stops stressing the importance of expanding boundaries and stretching our comfort zones until they lose their snap. He says to be ready to call anyone a brother, and his commands to parent kiddos who don't share our DNA are painfully unmuddy.

"Give justice to the poor and the orphan; uphold the rights of the oppressed and the destitute. Rescue the poor and helpless; deliver them from the grasp of evil people" (Ps. 82:3–4).

For all the times we accuse God of being mysterious or unclear, this isn't one of them. Jesus pointed to you and me and called us his brother/sister/mother. God in heaven looked out across the breadth of his chosen people, his "own," and said his heart would not be complete without adopting us into his clan and making us kin. This same God who designed the quirkiest, most wonderful family tree from an entire humanity of orphaned fugitives looks us squarely in the face and says he expects the same from us.

If we love him, we will do this. We will find a way to rescue the helpless. It would be easier if he'd hedged a bit, only using words like *care for*, *pray for*, or our flexible favorite, *love*, which can so easily be shaped out of a mud-on-our-boots, action-packed directive and into a mood of general agreeability. If we love salsa, sleeping in on Saturdays, and *Parks and Rec*, well, yes, we can also love orphans.

Instead he just goes for it. *Give. Uphold. Rescue. Deliver.* These are the verbs attached to God's intention for our care of orphans. He tells us to spend ourselves on their behalf, to let our arms grow tired from propping them up. We know all about spending, don't we? Empty our pockets. Bankrupt our time reserves. Pour it out, deplete the coffers, exhaust our limits, *spend*.

This doesn't mean every capable family is supposed to adopt a child. But each of us is charged with finding a way to partner with God and the work to ransom his people. This is something we *get* to do, our capacity to love expanded through his enduring love for us. Though we're prone to causing trouble and putting ourselves first, only because of God's refusal to take us at face value, he invites us to the party and gives us a first-row seat to the way he redeems a universe of orphaned souls into the treasured family of God.

We All Need a Haven (Both Kinds)

We shouldn't be surprised when a me-centric culture leads to a family-centric values system where family is unimaginatively defined only along bloodlines and a shared genetic code.

Even with the perspective of adoption on our side, Cory and I still needed help seeing beyond "us," our little family unit. Our instinct, just like that of most parents, was to circle in and hunker down. For all the heartbreak we felt along the road to starting a family, things had finally come together. We had cut a new groove, and loving my role as a mama was surprisingly disconnected from my apathy toward cats. With three kiddos at home under the age of six, one of whom was still mired in the sort of rage that threatened our resolve at times, our days weren't necessarily easy. But we'd pounded out a rhythm hatched of snacks, nap time (bless it!), and wrapping the table with Kraft paper in order to paint our blues away.

We were a family, and it didn't take long at all to be hyper-consumed with *us*. The work often felt mundane, but it was worthy. Though this wasn't our original plan, we adapted quickly, crooning along with Garth Brooks about unanswered prayers and the kind way God knows us better than we know ourselves. We hadn't chosen this path to family, but we wouldn't have changed it for anything.

Our family was complete, we decided, at least for a good, long while. Our hearts and hands were full. Seasoned experts on conventional wisdom, we recognized the signs. We'd reached our limit, and we knew God agreed.

Sometimes God speaks through unanswered prayers, and other times he straight up shocks us, answering prayers we never knew to pray. Reading one of my favorite novels late one night, inspired by the author, I made the offhand remark to Cory, "If we ever have another daughter, we should name her Haven." Two months later, paving more road along our continual redemption,

God sent a blond-haired teenager to the door of our farmhouse. She had been disappointed on repeat, let down by everyone, including herself. And her name was Haven. We'd been wrong again. We weren't maxed out after all. Rather, God moved in to our slim reserves and showed us he had plans for us. With Haven, we touched the edges of what it meant to spend ourselves for the sake of a stranger.

She was sullen, shifty, and dramatic. She was polite, for the most part, but kept to herself and slept the days away. Often it was like she wasn't even there.

We naively assumed she'd be drawn into our functional, relatively peaceful family dynamic. Of course she wouldn't be able to resist us.

Instead she hung back while we struggled to define our role in her life.

She resisted our wisdom and remained steadfastly immune to the ease of our boring routine. She proved difficult to reach. I didn't have a clue how to love her. I imagined late-night talks, board games, and wholesome television with salty bowls of popcorn. Maybe I would teach her to cook. Maybe our structure would be contagious, biting her resolve when her defenses were worn and dull.

What happened instead was disgruntled dinners around a table where her cell phone was banned and the food wasn't always to her liking. There were truckloads of drama and tears, both real and fake. Cory and I grew comfortable admitting we had no idea which ones were which.

And we were no better.

My help was often veiled in martyrdom, quietly stewing

in the suffering my sacrifice required and impatiently awaiting my overdue pat on the back. We lit all the wrong fuses, waged passive-aggressive turf wars, and kept score.

God reached out and squared our shoulders to this daughter whom he loved with an intensity that matched his love for us. We were pulled at the ends, thin and weary in the middle, but without realizing it, we grew protective of her. And every late night spent talking about things that mattered was worth ten angsty nights. Tired and exasperated, we found ourselves wanting to defend her cause in spite of ourselves. We wanted to turn back time for her or zoom the reel past what we knew was ahead of her.

Once strangers, we invited her into our home, and she invited us into her life. Our decision to belong to each other was mutual. It wasn't always easy, but it mattered in ways none of us understood. We couldn't have imagined the way our relationship would continue to deepen and unfold over the next five years or how she would sometimes forget and call us Mom and Dad. At the time we were practicing our obedience, attaching training wheels to the unsteady idea that maybe we were useful to the kingdom in the midst of our everyday lives. For one of the first times ever, a need presented itself, and we simply responded. *Yes.*

This is what our faith requires, to not close our eyes to an open door. God is found in the homeless stranger, the hunger-cramped neighbor, the thirsty traveler, the shackled and forgotten. "'For I was hungry, and you fed me. . . . I was a stranger, and you invited me into your home. I was naked, and you gave me clothing. I was sick, and you cared for me. I was in prison, and you visited me'" (Matt. 25:35–36).

It was hard to paint Haven as one of the elusive ones Jesus

says to love as his proxy, the stranger, the naked, the sick, the imprisoned. She had things like a smartphone and pocket money, not to mention two parents. She wore braces, for crying out loud.

And yet she was the gift of God sent to our door. Before long others followed her path, broken-down teenagers in name-brand shoes with shirts that matched their hats.

At first most of them didn't fit the frame.

But I watched the ways the world hated them, deciding they'd never amount to anything. And I watched the ways the world loved them, easy targets for its apple-cheeked lies.

My lens was shifting, its range ballooning.

God was showing us the way he owned all our days and how each one of these teenagers, these sons and daughters, held an opportunity for us to love him by loving his people. Though at this point in our journey we were finally ready to do something outlandish and extreme for God, he asked to be paid instead in long stretches where life sounded like a whisper and our offerings were small.

After all the brouhaha of putting our house on the market and getting ready to pitch ourselves straight into something strange and new, the housing market languished and we waited. The currency God would eventually ask of us would be big moves, wide-open minds, and neighbors whose lives would intersect ours in ways that changed us forever. Until then, it was an extra hour in the van as we drove Haven to school or soccer practice, a bowl of soup at the end of a long day, reality TV (the great unifier of generations!), and the grace to simply remember the fragile intentions of a teenager.

This is how the kingdom of heaven comes down sometimes,

in small moments where we can choose to believe he makes much of little, in ordinary pockets where what feels like waiting is actually the undercover work of our resolve being steeled for what waits for us.

The Mama Type

The first time I met the next kid who would become my own, it was January and he wasn't wearing a coat.

Cory had met him through the alternative high school where Cory had worked as an administrator. Though this kid was funny and engaging, his fuse was always half-lit and his downward spiral greased and ready.

He had no close family connections and his birthday was around the corner, so we decided to take him to a sit-down-and-order restaurant for his first time.

His name was Robert, and that's all I knew.

The thing about me is, I'm just no good in unfamiliar situations. I'm allergic to small talk and terrified by the thought of causing or even bearing witness to someone else's emotional discomfort. If I detect even a hint of awkwardness, I amp it up. Somehow, I manage to make matters worse. I talk too much or clam up altogether. I leave the heavy lifting for someone else, even if "someone else" could only be my husband, who happens to be even worse at this sort of thing.

In terms of the potential for awkwardness or unmet expectations, taking a stranger out for his seventeenth birthday felt fairly monumental. On top of that, I just didn't get teenage boys. I had no clue what he would be like or how I would relate to him. I defaulted to sensationalized information gathered from pop culture and the media. What could possibly go wrong? Robert was mysterious to me. Mythical, even.

I wished God had given me a different personality, one better suited to this sort of thing. I pictured all the mama-types in the movies, quick with a hug, sincere, bosomy and safe, smelling faintly of flour, wearing nonthreatening mom jeans and maybe a perm.

I wasn't that person. I floundered in high-stakes conversation, physical affection with strangers made me twitchy, and my jeans were smack-dab in the middle of the Mom-Cool continuum. I couldn't decide on my angle. I wasn't technically old enough to be a mom figure, at least not according to my frame of reference at the time, but way too old to be relatable.

What if he was sullen? Rude? What if he cussed in front of the kids or texted all through dinner? The possibilities for failure were incalculable, but it didn't stop me from ticking down the list. By the time we arrived to pick him up, the whole event felt like *my* personal risk, and, quite honestly, I wanted to turtle into my puffy coat and hide.

Just as my well-honed flight response was kicking in, he slow-poked from the trailer where he'd been staying, wearing a red T-shirt covered in skulls, his bare skin fading into the darkness around him. Just like that, I loved him a little. Deep inside, under my protective layers and all my excuses, buried beneath my ignorance and pride, nearly suffocated by my false realities and unholy ideas, a brand-new spark was lit. The flame flickered small, barely breathing, but a part of me knew in that moment he belonged to us and my heart would never be the same.

He was poor.

He was, for all intents and purposes, an orphan.

But neither of those facts had any real bearing on why I was already tamping down the urge to mother him as we took our seats in the restaurant. My heart was not responding to the commandment from Psalm 82; it was reacting to the palpable presence of God pinging across that vinyl booth.

Never before, certainly not in adulthood, had I allowed room for this kind of movement of his spirit. I was accustomed to believing the Holy Spirit was mostly concerned with things like fasting and keeping a prayer journal. I assumed the instruction of the Spirit was more along the lines of "Pray on your actual knees, Shannan, instead of waiting until you're tucked into bed, half-asleep." I thought what God wanted was more spiritual discipline and less sin. It hadn't crossed my mind that obedience might mean spending an awkward evening with a teenager or springing for an overpriced slice of cheesecake. I'd never considered the sacrifice of risking my emotional equilibrium for the sake of another or offering my time to tangibly love a stranger with sad eyes.

Just a taste, *just one*, and I swallowed that hook. I gulped it down whole, feeling the pinch of the barb as it took permanent root. It felt like surgery, like a place inside me was being changed, extracted, added to, *something*.

If it was a little uncomfortable, it was only a prelude to everything that would happen next.

Jail Mom

One year later, Robert disappeared from our lives, gone without a word or shadow. When he reappeared seven months later, it was to tell us he would soon be the father of twin boys.

I drove him to the hospital to meet his sons on a sticky June evening.

Two months later, he was arrested and sent to jail.

God often shows us our purpose in quiet ways. We see a sliver here, a slice there. There are moments when our hearts thump in our chests, and we're left wondering what it means, patching his holiness over our humanity and seeing the way it gives shape to our tattered edges.

The day I sat in a courtroom, boring holes through his neck, his shoulders, his growing-out Afro, begging God to allow us just one silent moment of connection, I was never more sure of what I was created to do.

Emily P. Freeman wrote in her book, *A Million Little Ways*, "When we recognize the place where our desire runs parallel to that of Christ's, then we will live in the midst of the now-but-not-quite-yet with a peace that goes beyond our ability to understand."[1]

Sitting in that drab courtroom with its oppressively low ceiling, I wasn't thinking about visiting the "least of these" in jail, or defending the cause of the orphan, or even specifically about Jesus. My entire being was fixed on Robert, the frame of a man carting around the heart of a child. I listened, but only halfway. I'd heard it all before. I knew what those papers said, and to be honest I just didn't care. I had beheld Robert's wonder in flashes, a highlight reel of his disarming sweetness. I'd watched him braid the hair of a disabled three-year-old, making her somehow even cuter than she already was. I'd heard about him walking neighbor kids to the bus on their first day of school because their mom hadn't come home that morning. He took their picture with his flip phone and told them to have fun and listen to their teacher.

Now there he stood, shackled, in jail-issued pants that were six inches too short, meeting eyes with the judge who held his future, speaking softly and with humility. I was nervous for him, proud of him, scared to death for him. His shame was the cinder block of the walls, the concrete of the floors, the drab of the polyester, the bite of the shackles. It trailed behind him, emanated from him. It was tangible, heavy, something I could reach out and shove. I couldn't bear it. Unable to do anything else, I winked at him, smiling my smallest smile. He watched me, taking it in with eyes that had lost their light. And I knew for sure he owned the rest of my life, just like the three little ones waiting at home did. I rearranged the emotional furniture of my heart once again, shoving and scooting, widening the circle.

We kept returning to Robert, exhaling each time he returned again to us.

We couldn't undo the past, relive for him the day he landed in jail, or lean the scales more in mercy's favor, but we could drive to the county jail, send our shoes through the metal detector, and make him smile twice a week. We could show up at every court hearing—and be reprimanded by the officer for waving at the defendant. We could fill yellow legal pads with our high hopes for him and drop them in the mail. We could nearly bankrupt ourselves with overpriced jailhouse phone calls.

The trick-math of this upside-down Jesus economy promises that we can never outspend our reserves. There is no limit, only capacity.

When Robert was shipped off to prison, our pockets hung heavy with quarters for vending machine hot chips and Mountain Dew at our bimonthly visits. We became acquainted with a system that barks instead of speaks, where gentleness is lost and the lights stay on all night. We sat across from him at a rickety table in a visitation room that pulsed with solidarity among other families doing the same, meeting a loved one at his lowest place and rallying to keep his spirits lifted. Robert grew accustomed to his bunkmates' faces twisting in confusion when he said we were his parents. At the end of one visit, he risked a write-up and shouted from down the hall, "Mom! Mom! Aren't you my mom?" then nodded at the guy standing next to him. *Told ya.*

When his time had been served, they released him back into the world a changed man, for better and worse, with a GED certificate and the fresh coating of strange pride that a stint "upstate" will give a young man who cut his teeth on the streets. We waved him inside. The paint was barely dry on his room in our unfinished basement, and he was home. We spent the next seven months navigating the travails of parenting a kid who was technically an adult, one who wasn't accustomed to rules, expectations, or food that didn't come from a bag.

He was thrust into the role of single parent to two active one-year-old boys, and they joined us a couple of nights each week. As difficult as it already was to know our place with Robert, finding the lines as we watched him instinct-parent his babies in our kitchen felt like an exercise in extreme futility. Add to that the fact that we were all sharing one computer (with no Wi-Fi—house arrest rules) and that he'd decided to go cold turkey on cigarettes, and you see this soup I'm stirring: a recipe for disaster.

There were arguments, slammed doors (him), tears (he says I'm a crybaby), and so many apologies and do-overs. At every turn, God flipped my indignation around, holding it as a mirror before my own beady browns. *I have so much more for you than your tired, stubborn ways, Shannan.*

Those early months together felt like rending of heart from flesh, constantly stepping past myself, then retreating again. I was all questions and no good answers. From the vantage point of parenting a kid who might as well have been raised on a different planet, I began to question every bit of the middle-class wisdom I'd learned by osmosis.

But when I tell you it was hard, I'm not done talking.

There was also so much good.

Like how I'd wake before dawn to hear his boots across the kitchen floor, and the universe couldn't contain my pride for my hardworking son. I'd listen to him coo at his boys, and my heart would split at the seams. One time he "fried up" a bunch of potatoes with the fanciest bottle of olive oil I'll ever own. Another time he enacted a boil-bake combo-of-doom with a New York strip steak he found in our freezer, and I came face-to-face with my stingy, inflexible heart. I'm laughing now, but I acted like a petty child at the time. *My precious, highbrow olive oil! Why do you hate me?*

He taught me I can never be good enough, middle-class enough, or faithful enough to change someone's eternity. It's not my job. Never was. There were laughs. And plenty of nonsense. He taught me to be a better listener and the importance of saying, "I was wrong." He continues to teach me about unconditional love and my fundamental need for grace, reminding me that my worst moment doesn't define me. He shows me how to bend low to rise up.

We can't give him back his first twenty-one years. We can't unstitch old wounds or paint him a rosier future. We sure as heck can't hand him eternity or make him want our faith.

But we can love him with a love that doesn't stop trying and hope it matters.

We can prove again that he can't outrun his chances, no matter how many times he moves in and out of our home.

We can mend our broken places into a blanket that covers all of us and call it a family.

Belong to Me

Two nights ago we celebrated Ruby's ninth birthday. Our mode of "celebrating" birthdays is epically low-key. I hang the birthday banner, made years ago from two tubes of paint and some cheap paper plates. The cake is usually from a box. We huddle around one of our great loves to say, "We're so glad you were born." Who cares if the house is a mess? So what if dinner is a giant grocery-store pizza?

One thing I've learned about parenting brokenhearted kids is that you can expect to have your heart broken in the process. It's the sort of ache that finds you climbing to a top bunk after midnight, curling your shape around an exhausted child who sometimes has trouble warding off the pain of early losses. It's the perpetual slap of rejection from a child who loves you so much and cannot make sense of his anger. These are contact burns—the white-hot pain of those around us singeing our own skin. It's real and it's complicated, and it makes me feel alone. Sometimes, it's hard not to be numb.

But hope always comes in the morning, and it usually takes a different form than the one I expect. Ruby's little "party" was a distinct relief at the end of a crushing string of weeks.

Our family had grown into a mash-up of bloodlines and heartstrings and "you belong to me"s. We crowded into the kitchen, along with Robert, his then-girlfriend Charity, and two of her kids, Jordyn and Kayley. Haven joined us, along with her daughter, Avery. We gathered around the table to celebrate Ruby River, the best nine-year-old alive—daughter/sister/friend to the end.

When I had asked Robert if they wanted to come for the party, he cocked his head to the side and actually said, *"Duh."* When Ruby found out who was coming, she cheered. This is the family my children know, the one that continues to sprout up like patches of wild clover and bloom into something bigger and more fully "us." Their delineations of "sister" and "brother" are pliable, but sturdy.

My kids, each of whom made profound sacrifices on their way to forever, know a thing or two about the hard roads that intersect at family. They have seen firsthand the short path between stranger and beloved.

All of us have been fundamentally shaped by the reality that when it comes to love, there is no limit. Love is never divided. It always, always multiplies. In this modern-day economy where resources eventually deplete and spending leads to deficits, we know we've landed safely at this secret place where, yet again, conventional wisdom bows to the ridiculous hopefulness of Immanuel.

The evening of the party, in the best possible showing of good faith, everyone arrived on time. Avery ran for me, shouting, with all the hopped-up, three-year-old enthusiasm her chubby little toddler bod holds. Ruby and Jordyn got comfy at the dining room table with a can of markers and plain paper.

Cory hauled in a stack of pizza boxes, dodging Silas, who buzzed through the kitchen at a rate of speed that rendered him a blur, with the volume level of a beginner's bagpipe brigade. Kayley watched quietly from Charity's arms.

Calvin stayed close to the action, never wanting to stray far from his big brother, the best version of a superhero imaginable. Robert and Haven clowned around about their hair (Robert obsesses about his hair always—it's a whole "thing") and launched into their go-to brand of drama-talk. So-and-so had gotten locked up. Someone was pregnant. And all kinds of people were "trippin'."

We downed slices of pizza and salt 'n' vinegar chips, grabbed hunks of watermelon from the bowl, spilled drinks, cleaned up messes, and defused more than one fight between the little ones. When it was time to sing, I promise you, you have never heard a sorrier version of "Happy Birthday," halting and way off-key.

We played a few heated rounds of a board game, and before he left, Robert gave Ruby a dollar. She didn't stop beaming the entire night. This was her family, or at least many of us, crammed into a small space, talking over each other, laughing and scrapping as every family does.

It was the kind of chaos that comes scary-close to giving me a cluster headache but mercifully veers off at the last moment into frazzled, bone-deep gratitude.

Family is rooted in forever, hardwired with the sort of love that won't ever give up and views the past as just a step along the road to what's permanent. Its shape isn't static. It bends and blurs and keeps time with the rhythm of an open door. *You are welcome here.* One person leads to another, and then to the next. We have family who lives with us, family down the street and across town, family we see every day, every week, or when they've missed the bus and need a ride.

I'm not sure when "we" will be complete, and I'm throwing my chips on never. There's no easy way to say anymore who belongs to me and who doesn't. It's not up to me. It never was.

Our tree grows, its branches jutting out at odd angles. If given a thousand tries, I couldn't have come up with something as perfect as us. We are in this for keeps, imperfect and bumbling on the job, at our best when we circle up for cheap pizza and store-bought cake.

On Big Kids

Now and then I'm asked what it's like to adopt, and people especially wonder about adopting big kids from hard places. Some might say I'm a fool and I'm putting my family at risk. Every once in a while I lock eyes with someone, and it's clear—they want a big, weird family of their own.

Here's what I would say to that: this sort of family, cobbled together from necessity and the stubborn insistence that God wasn't playing when he said no one should be left lonely, it will unhinge you.

These big kids, they will wreck you.

They won't always be as grateful as you hope and will expose your own selfishness. They'll storm off when you tell them the truth about things. They'll smoke on your front porch. They'll tell you lies.

They'll hog the couch and make you laugh when you're trying to read. They'll eat nasty food. They'll teach you things you never wanted to know about a life you couldn't possibly have imagined.

They'll find the loosest seam of your heart, and they'll yank that thread.

They'll exhaust you, exasperate you. They'll crack you up so bad.

They'll go home. Go to jail. Go missing for months on end. They'll avoid your calls. They'll unfriend you.

You'll tell yourself you're done, then wonder where they're sitting as the moon lifts higher.

You'll worry every single day about them and pray that they come back.

You'll have a front-row seat to many of their failures, but you just won't care too much about the mistakes. You only want them safe under your roof. You want to feed them peanut butter cake and heat them a bowl of soup.

At every turn you'll see yourself in them and wonder how anyone was ever able to put up with you. You'll be unable to ignore the ways you settle for less than you were made for, align with lies, and struggle to live as a child of God.

You'll find something to be proud of and say it often and out loud—*"I'm proud of you."* You'll learn a tiny bit about the complicated codes they live and love by.

Your heart will break in shock waves, a second time, a tenth.

It won't matter. You'll love them.

Here, in this land of the messy, grumpy, nit-picking living, my long-term plans continue to be stunningly wrong. Life keeps turning me on a dime, then doing it again. Every time I land, the sky is green, the earth is blue, and I'm slack-jawed over the good sense it makes.

In this wonky approach to knitting our family together, we didn't actually solve anyone's problems. It was never about that. We just kept the door ajar, and they walked in. And then we didn't want them to leave.

Dr. Phil says hurt people *hurt* people, and I've seen it in action, from both sides. But standing at my kitchen island with my ragtag band of comrades, I'm inclined to believe the opposite is true too. We're all hurting, to varying depths. Some wounds bear more indelible manifestations; these scars can't be covered. We don't need fresh air or increased personal space in order to heal. We need the gentle compression of each other, living in close proximity with certain kinship. Hurt people *heal* people.

Offer love and acceptance, and it will circle back around. Do this, and "your gift will return to you in full—pressed down, shaken together to make room for more, running over, and poured into your lap. The amount you give will determine the amount you get back" (Luke 6:38).

Family was meant to live on a loop, a hazy beginning with no end in sight, the pulsing bass line that God's kingdom on earth is alive. Right here.

3

HAVE LESS

Earthly possessions dazzle our eyes and delude us into think-
ing that they can provide security and freedom from anxiety.
Yet all the time they are the very source of all anxiety.
—*The Cost of Discipleship*, Dietrich Bonhoeffer[1]

AT THIRTY-NINE YEARS of age, I've learned a hearty sum of
important things, all of which have proved useful at key moments
in my life. Aside from learning to walk and the impossible
miracle of language acquisition, I've learned to read, tie my
shoes, ride a bike, and cook a mean marinara with meatballs—
throw in a handful of capers, and tell me it doesn't change your
culinary worldview. I've learned how to plan a gallery wall, write
a sonnet, whisk together a basic vinaigrette, and shoot a free
throw. Somewhere along the way, I also learned to administer
the Heimlich maneuver and used it for all it was worth when
Silas, at age two, inhaled a cheese stick.

There are plenty of things I didn't learn, like how to do a

perfect cartwheel, change a flat tire, or play chess. One of my greatest regrets is that I never *really* learned how to swim.

In spite of these learning deficits, my life has been both manageable and robust. Chagrined as my grandma would be, my inability to bake a proper piecrust hasn't killed my joy or sequestered me from my life goals. I haven't suffered for most of my failings.

But unlike domestic shortcomings or my global coordination deficiencies (think every sport known to man, all forms of dance, and that thing where you pat your head and rub your stomach at the same time), some life skills have much higher stakes, one in particular being the management of money.

I never learned the right way to do this, at least not in a way that best honors God and the job he gave me to love my neighbor as I love myself.

I'm truly sorry to have to bring money into this discussion. Talking about it is tremendously awkward for everyone. It makes us squirrelly, and it doesn't even matter which direction the conversation veers. I wish it were a nonissue, that the journey to more surrender and more Jesus didn't have to include a tug-of-war over a couple of zeroes. If it were up to me, I would omit this niggling chapter from my story. Sadly, there's just no way I could leave it out and maintain even a shred of authenticity or integrity. It remains a struggle.

No matter who we are or how much we have, handling our money in the weird way of Jesus will probably not come naturally. It'll require some major demo of our old ideas. I so badly want to look you in the eye and tell you we're all doing fine, then ride the status quo like a wave. It would just feel better that way.

But I know Jesus made people squirm whenever he mentioned money, and if the people of his day needed a firm talking-to, then you and I are well past due. So, let's go ahead and rip the Band-Aid off. Let's handle this like I do every episode of *The Bachelor*—with my eyes half-covered, so itchy and uncomfortable that I can't possibly turn away.

Financial Freedom

I spent most of my adult life believing I was some kind of fiscal-responsibility poster child. I did what I was told, and then some. I read books by experts. I tithed. I was confident in my strategy, and the nods of approval affirmed my hunches.

In reality, my heart and my head were inverted when it came to money. I screwed it up but appeared to the world around me like a rip-roaring success. I did it "right" but got it all wrong.

It wasn't for a lack of trying.

I was trained, well taught. I learned to balance a checkbook, avoid credit cards, live below my means, and save for the future. As bona fide adults, Cory and I signed up for classes that would fill in any gaps. We didn't buy designer jeans or roll around town in a flashy ride. But under the surface of our "financial steward-ship" lurked a breathless love affair with our bank account balance. This true condition of our hearts was one of our best-kept secrets.

The more we had, the more we wanted. The taller the stack grew, the more focused we became on protecting it. We prided ourselves on letting our small children run carefree and un-attended through our pastures while we helicopter-parented our bank accounts, circling in, constantly hovering and checking, our stomachs lurching when the stock market dipped.

We had our reasons. What we wanted, maybe more than anything else, was freedom. That seemed to be the goal of the successful people around us, the ones pushing us to earn more, save more, "retire a millionaire." We wanted to be like them. We wanted suntanned faces and a breeze on our skin—the easy life. Who wanted a life of stress or angst? Not us. We wanted the sunset slipping down the horizon line—a hope that belonged to us. We wanted unshackled hearts, the ability to sail away or stay.

Research says most couples fight about money, but that wasn't true in our case. We had a plan, and if we kept working it, we told ourselves, we'd eventually be financially set. Our hearts called us to an intangible something that would untangle our knotted places and drift us to sleep at the end of the day. All we wanted was freedom.

We assumed it could be bought.

In our combined sixty-plus years of following Jesus, we hadn't received the clear message that true financial freedom is found not by storing up, safeguarding, or protecting our cash like a tiny, cooing baby.

In fact, the only way to experience financial freedom is to be freed from the finances.

It sounds so simple. And frankly, so wrong.

Webster's dictionary defines freedom as "liberation from slavery or restraint."[2] Having parented our oldest child through his incarceration, the words aren't lost on us.

It's almost comical now that what we thought was the key to freedom involved password-protected accounts, neck-tied advisors, and armored trucks. This false freedom required us to be deeply committed to its growth, to keep our eyes fixed on it—our prize. The precise number on the balance didn't matter, as long as it was steadily rising. Growth was the goal, and we guarded it with our lives. To do anything else would mean losing.

The Shiniest Loot

One perpetual problem of my life is my fundamental insistence on defining the world in human terms and conditions. Jesus said the first would be last and the least was the favored one, but I'm a sensible woman of the twenty-first century. I've built half a life on the back of my ability to compartmentalize, so I shelve the Bible over there while I live over here.

The only way to keep this house of cards from toppling is to frame certain portions as strictly parabolic, wiggling my way around its literal application to my life. There's simply too much to lose.

It seems impossible that God would prefer that we let go of our excess or descend from the rungs of our handcrafted success. We prefer a message of financial prosperity, imagining a God who might allow us to be the one camel who slips through the eye of the needle. Meanwhile, Jesus warns that wherever our treasure is, *that's* where our heart is (Matt. 6:21). In pursuit of our hearts, he reminds us that his is tethered to relationships, not things.

Yet, for so much of my life, my heart lived somewhere in an intangible fund and on printed-off statements. My secret identity was a dollar amount.

Cory and I belonged to our money. *We* were our shiniest treasure.

What we called freedom was really self-proud independence in disguise. We wanted to owe nothing, depend upon no one.

We wanted to be the boss of our lives, never stopping to consider that our perspective ran contrary to the fundamentals of the faith we said governed us.

Though we all know folks who prove it's possible to have financial wealth yet not be enslaved by it, they appear to be the minority, and Cory and I didn't fall neatly into their camp. We had much compared to many, and very little compared to some. But viewed from either angle, we were jailbirds.

So God hoisted a wrecking ball and aimed it toward our captivity.

In his usual ankles-up, what-just-happened way, he skipped logic and convention and met us right where we were, back on the farm, doing our best to raise our three small kids. He messed with the boring basics of our lives in order to prove his larger point.

When the dust settled and we uncovered our eyes, it was blindingly clear: the only way to be free was to open our hands and let God decide what stayed up and what needed to fall. Our retinas burned for days.

The Ministry of Robot Teeth

I used to have big ideas about kids with silver teeth. I'm embarrassed to admit it, but I once believed, in all my stunning arrogance, silver baby teeth were the hallmark of a particularly grim parental failure.

You can imagine my horror when I toted my darling five-year-old to the dentist only to be told he had a cavity.

Fine, he had twelve.

And four of them needed root canals.

There were four shiny, silver, baby chompers directly in my future, and I'd never felt more abandoned by God.

The whole ordeal ignited a tremendous amount of shame in me. I was ashamed of being ashamed, and then I went ahead and became ashamed of the way my new shame made me feel about the way I used to secretly shame others. Enough shame for everyone, but mostly for me.

Because of the gravity of the situation, the dentist planned to wheel our tiny son into surgery, anesthetize him, and do the necessary work in one fell swoop while I pretended to read a paperback in the hospital waiting room. This is who I had become and where I found myself.

On top of the internal struggle, there was the cash. *Nelly, back it up.*

The only thing they needed from us was four thousand dollars.

While it wasn't exactly a day at the circus to confront my ugly disposition for casting judgment, this was actual, paper money. And that's a whole 'nother thing.

It didn't matter that we had our Dave Ramsey emergency fund to draw from; I was outraged that *this* was our emergency.

I wanted to decide.

I wanted control.

It was bad enough that God had allowed this, but making us hand over part of our beloved emergency fund? Well, that was asking too much.

Allow me to point out the obvious: I thought this was sort of the end. Not in a "we won't survive this" way, but it felt pretty bleak. Standing on this side of reason, it seems ridiculous. But at the time, it was everything. What today sounds like a silly story about a spoiled girl felt like a visceral unhinging at the time. My life was so falsely insulated and secure, and the reins seemed to fit so nicely in my hand, but it didn't take much to pitch me straight to the ground.

In hindsight, I'm pretty glad I didn't lose my faith over this one. It seems like it wouldn't have been worth it.

Our son emerged from surgery with "robot teeth" (side note: five-year-olds have a contagious glass-half-full approach that makes me envious), a constant and visible reminder of the ways I had lost control of my life.

For the next month we watched our well-appointed financial stability continue to trickle from our life via an unholy trinity of home repairs, car trouble, and income taxes, all usual suspects, yet not things I'd ever seen as instruments of God's sanctification.

Somewhere along the way, I had a moment of clarity.

It didn't happen when I was reading my Bible or praying. It happened when I was lamenting the strange state of things with a long-distance friend, from the safety of my reasonable, risk-free, beige couch.

"I think God wants us to get rid of our money."

The words didn't trip out of my mouth as much as they flew. Though they came from my lips, they were not from my heart.

For all the years we'd spent crediting our success and capability to our unfussy upbringings, our college degrees, our gutsiness, our intellect, our work ethic, our wisdom, and our restraint, Jehovah Jireh, God our provider, had stood by and watched us "humbly" accept the glory for what we believed was financial wisdom and good stewardship. We were quick to assume he'd allowed us these blessings, never considering the day might come when he would trade them for better ones.

Surrounded for most of our lives by people just like us, we had enjoyed the ease of our shared middle-class vernacular. Filtering in from every side was the blandly uniform message: work hard, save hard, spend in cash. The gospel on finances had been reduced to three clear tenets: (1) don't live in debt, (2) tithe 10 percent, and (3) save for the future. We weren't trying to keep up with the Joneses as much as we were constantly reassuring ourselves *we* were still Joneses.

Along with most of the modern-day church, Cory and I whitewashed the warning against "the love of money" into "the love for *someone else's* money" (debt). It served us well.

But, oh, we loved our money. We did so "responsibly"; some might even say, "Christianly." We thought we could love our cash as much as we wanted to, as long as it was *our* cash. We gave ourselves every gift we ever wanted and said they were from God.

The part we somehow missed was that our money wasn't ours. And it had never been.

I wish there were some wiggle room. Regrettably, God is achingly clear about the relationship between us and our stuff.

For starters, "No one can serve two masters. For you will hate one and love the other; you will be devoted to one and despise the other. You cannot serve God and be enslaved to money" (Matt. 6:24).

In case you're interested, here's how I wormed my way around that one for, oh, thirty-odd years: I swore I didn't serve money.

Boom. So easy.

Never mind that my life didn't align with this working theory I'd spun from thin air. Unquestionably, I spent far more time and concern on things related to cash than on things related to the kingdom. Still, I stitched my little white lie onto the fabric of my heart.

Let's take my general greed and my more specific lust for things like department store makeup or a wardrobe that would require its own little room with its own light switch. Let's stir in my longing for a house large enough to realistically shelter a small tribe of people. Let's mix together every ugly thing I'm baring, and let's boil it all down: I forgot this world isn't my home. This ground I walk on is not the one I was made for. And because that's true, nothing I hold on earth is worthy of eternity. My finances aren't a gift as much as a loan. A means to an end. An opportunity to invest in eternity, not a deed ascribing my status in a world where I'm supposed to be a stranger.

This wasn't a super-intentional disobedience. I simply found it easier to stay lost and uninformed in my middle-class Land of Plenty than risk acknowledging the ways I was wrong.

It got worse: "Whoever loves money never has enough; whoever loves wealth is never satisfied with their income" (Eccl. 5:10 NIV).

It didn't matter that we'd reached a certain benchmark in our minds. We live in the twenty-first century, where financial success is short-lived if it doesn't keep growing. The beast must be fed.

Here's how I made friends with this elephant in the room: I found a creative way to make my yearning for more money a "righteous" intention.

I wore my excess like a holy sister's habit, vowing that if God would allow us to keep earning more income, we would give more away. God could surely use more wealthy tithers in his world-saving toolbox. Why not us?

It sounded innocent enough, but the root was that I just wanted more money. *Keep the floodgates open, God, and we'll continue to share with you.*

I wanted a reasonable justification for staying rich. I didn't want to suffer at all for charity. I didn't want to know what it felt like to sacrifice, though, in my mind, I *would* be sacrificing. I would be sacrificing things I never planned to have in the first place. Something like, "I could be driving around in a brand-new Toyota, but instead I'm still in my beat-up Ford Explorer. I could have a complicated satellite TV package, but instead I rage against the finicky rabbit ears, feeling forgotten by the modern age. See how I sacrifice for the poor?"

I killed two birds with one stone.

I sacrificed nothing at all but went to bed at night convinced I had.

Graciously, God loved us too much to let us continue wasting precious years of this oh-so-long life coveting ash and rust.

The more we studied and prayed, the harder it got to reconcile a large bank account with a world that dies while we sleep. The blinders that had long protected our American Dream from the trauma of the gospel were falling off. We were not living a life worthy of God's calling. Our excuses were wrung limp. We had to choose a new path, and though the Holy Spirit was doing his work in our hearts, our feet had to move. Time was wasting. The questions of our hearts became, for the first time, *What can we do? How can we walk a different way?*

As we began to understand the need for change, we saw that these burgeoning questions had already been answered.

Drop the Jar

God sent his beloved boy to the earth to make a way for us, his other, infinitely more troublesome beloveds. The endgame has always been our eternal rescue, a future where our muddy shoes will hit streets of gold and be made holy.

Every day Jesus walks our way, seeing us not as we are right now but as who we are becoming. He offers us exactly what we need, but it doesn't fit the template we're expecting and our eyes strain to focus. He provides a better way, and we have the gall to say, "No. You're wrong." Everyone else is louder, from the Internet to the preachers to our wise Uncle Sam. We trade truth for noise.

If it's any consolation, this phenomenon doesn't belong solely to the modern age. As proficient as we are at complicating life, we aren't the first generation to choose poorly.

The day Jesus needed a drink on his way to Galilee, there was more at play than Sychar's arid climate. Legs aching, throat dry, he walked alone toward Jacob's well. The Samaritan woman watched him, wondering when he would catch his mistake and reroute. He was a Jew, and Jews didn't mingle with people like her. A few more steps, and she couldn't help wondering out loud, "What on earth do you want from me?"

What looked like his need was actually a plot point in her liberation. We know this story, that he offered her living water, the kind that would quench the thirst of her soul. We know that when faced with salvation, she dropped her water jug and ran in the direction of eternity.

But it's her line of questioning in the middle of the action that interests me.

"But sir, you don't have a rope or a bucket," she said, "and this well is very deep. Where would you get this living water? And besides, do you think you're greater than our ancestor Jacob, who gave us this well? How can you offer better water than he and his sons and his animals enjoyed?" (John 4:11–12)

I'm drawn to her words, because they have formed the low-pulsing rhythm of my own bullish, puffed-up heart.

God, you aren't handing me a plush retirement account or cash for the braces two-thirds of our kids inevitably will need. You don't have cheap health insurance for us, and this life is very long. You say this is freedom, so why am I wringing my hands in the dark? And besides, do you think you're wiser than financial planners or all our elders who tell us this road is too risky? Do you think you're smarter than my own dad? How can you possibly offer better water than our ancestors, who have handed down the currency of independence and personal provision like a birthright?

I can't say for sure what it takes to convince a stubborn, middle-class Jesus girl that his wisdom wraps far past the edges of her own.

But just like that scandalous woman who dropped her jug and ran, I'm beginning to find freedom in low places, even when no one around me understands, even when I'm confused or uncertain myself.

Jesus didn't unfurl a blueprint for the woman's future across the dirt by Jacob's well. He didn't answer any of her long-burning questions. He sure didn't promise her ease, stability, or financial prosperity.

He looked past who she was, with all her lovers and secrets, past her reputation, past the pretty face that must have made her infamous. He saw an empty woman, in need of him. He traded her doubts for a promise. He smiled in the face of her oddly type-A questioning about his lack of supplies and her street-weary skepticism, and saw his daughter.

In that moment, she recognized the heart of her dad.

Nothing else mattered. The past that imprisoned her was loosed. The water jar in her hands—her very livelihood—instantly became irrelevant, just like Peter's fishing nets. In order to inhabit the freedom offered by the walking, talking, recklessly loving Son of the living God, she first had to let go of the relics she thought made her free. In the time it took her shame to be painted over with grace, everything else she held became a non-treasure. It didn't matter what became of that jar. She dropped it to the ground.

And she ran. Straight into his mission.

God transformed this woman, despised and used, into his unlikely messenger. He invited her into a sacred place of worship and didn't mind at all that she came bearing some residual doubt. "Could he possibly be the Messiah?" (v. 29).

He invites us also into his curious existence and offers to lighten our load so we can finally touch freedom. We'll know it when we see it. Our hearts were created to track it down. He points us toward home, and though we may know little else, we know it's where we belong.

The Unraveling

Not long after the plug was pulled on our emergency savings, we were broadsided with a fast-moving series of what felt like tremendously unfortunate events.

Though for seven years I had worked part-time from our home since moving back to Indiana from Washington, DC, it was no surprise when the government contract I worked under came to an end following a change in the presidential administration. In fact, we breathed a collective sigh of relief. In the month that Silas had been home, it had become obvious that it no longer made sense for me to continue working in any capacity.

We accepted this transition as God's graciousness, allowing me to easily bow out of a career that had, up to that point, made more sense to hold on to. Still, my earnings accounted for exactly half of our household income. It was a blow to our finances, but we would be okay. Our family and the emotional health of our children were far more valuable, and Cory still earned plenty.

But when Cory, a top-level aide for a United States congressman, turned on the TV exactly one month later, just in time to see the headline that his boss was abruptly resigning from office amid that stale, old story line of scandal, we weren't quite as optimistic.

I was ashamed of the way my heart instantly seized in fear the morning we got the news. It was one of those "Honey, are you sitting down?" conversations that ended with an emotional blitz of fear, anger, confusion, and panic. I flung myself facedown on our bed after we hung up and wept in the sort of dramatic display I'd always frowned upon. My mind reeled, compulsively spinning the roulette wheel with all our chips on black, but knowing every slot was red. What were we going to do? Red. What about insurance? What about our sick kid? What about our growing family? Our adoption debt? Our mortgage? The rest of our entire lives? Red. Red. Red. Red.

We were sunk. The magnitude of our bad luck was staggering. On top of everything else, we were now entirely jobless.

In the coming weeks we kept two fingers pressed against the pulse of our bottom line. Having grown accustomed to a generous salary, we knew maximizing Cory's earning potential was mandatory. It suddenly didn't matter that our hearts were inching away from the more-is-more mind-set. Our reality demanded a new level of vigilance and thrift.

It's one thing to decide you can live with less when the cupboards and accounts are full. It's quite another when you've just been sucker punched, and the zeroes are falling down and rolling away like loosed marbles.

In stripping us of some of our wealth, God exposed our middle-class entitlement and the ways we were sunk in privilege. There we stood, in our spiritual skivvies, while he shifted our priorities every step of the way, allowing us less and less financial standing. Slowly, we began to see him at work in a situation where we once would have imagined his face turned away, silent and unhelpful.

On the one hand, it was the best kind of spiritual sugar rush—the crackling, electric sense that God was up to something. It felt like being picked for the team or followed on Twitter by a bigwig.

On the other hand, I missed my money, man.

I had thought for sure I was on my way to luxurious Nars and Aveda status, so what on earth was I doing back under the haze of discount Suave hairspray, which still smelled distinctly of the nineties, my lips lined with an unfortunately-named Wet *n* Wild lip pencil, #666? (You know a brand is down on its luck when it can't even afford to properly name its products.)

We declared certain months "no spend" zones, banning all restaurants, even Taco Bell, and if you know me at all, you might imagine the pain this caused me. During no-spend February, scheduled for the shortest month with great intention, I found myself living in a beautiful farmhouse lit with three-hundred-dollar floor lamps but eating a turkey sandwich in my car on the way to meet friends at the movies, the ticket for which they bought out of pity. Could I have afforded, say, a Burrito Supreme from the Taco Bell drive-thru? Of course. But I'd made it a matter of principle, based in large part on what I consider my noble amount of bullishness, along with the fact that I knew a slippery slope when I saw one. Oh, what tangled webs I weave when first I practice to make one teeny, tiny fast-food exception.

As our finances continued their lurchy descent, each bend in the road biting away at our income, I rose up against the establishment in ways both subtle and overly dramatic. In a bid to shake my material cravings, I canceled all the catalogs that arrived at my door and began tracking our cash budgeting system with Liam Neeson intensity. I strong-armed my fifty-dollar weekly grocery budget into a game culminating in my blog series I named "Grocery Store Confessional," which detailed each receipt in its totality. And I wasn't above secretly scanning our debit card records, trying to catch Cory buying Dunkin' Donuts coffee without reporting it. Times felt tough, and that was before our small-town postmistress openly taunted me for digging a ten out of an envelope labeled "miscellaneous" to buy a lavish full book of stamps.

Yet all the while, I remained solidly middle-class.

Please, go ahead, roll your eyes. My inability to adapt to less cash was profoundly inane. We can thank our misguided culture for my melodrama. What felt like far too little was actually still more than enough. I had to choose between fresh cherries and blackberries, not food and heat.

God shifted my thinking, and I slowly began to get over myself. Though I didn't necessarily enjoy the financial upheaval and couldn't see the larger picture, Cory and I recognized hope when we saw it and were shocked that it looked nothing like what we expected. Jesus' pull was compelling. Magnetic. It was impossible to argue with the man who so pointedly said, "Life is not measured by how much you own" (Luke 12:15) and who lived as a homeless refugee.

He freed us outright from the spiritual bondage of cushy jobs that allowed us to believe we could handle things ourselves. Other times, he simply offered a better way, and we could choose to either obey or ignore. God pointed us toward home, and we dropped our jar and ran. Once our hands were emptied, just like the woman at the well, our impulse was to run screaming through the streets. It felt like cracking an ancient code, and there was simply no alternative to being keyed up and crazy about it. God's more is actually less. Who would've guessed?

Once that jar hit the dirt, the gates swung open and the razor wire lost its sharp edges. We were free. Free to contribute more to things that mattered. Free to buy a cheaper house on the wrong side of the tracks so that we could actually meet the neighbors God said to love. Cory was free to jump off the ladder of perpetual financial momentum, moving from the security of politics to a job at a nonprofit alternative high school. We were beginning to understand the freedom to have less and do more.

Build the Roof

In the years following our liberation, the conversation has taken a hard swerve from "How much is too much?" to "How much is enough?" I have to say, it's a better place to be. We're past asking what's "responsible" or "safe." I don't care anymore what conventional wisdom or your whip-smart Uncle Ray might advise.

The Jesus I'm getting to know capsized conventional wisdom and lavished the poor with love. He tells me not to worry about the shirts in my closet or the cereal in my pantry. He invented cotton *and* oats. He owns the patents.

My Jesus blesses the poor and spits out what the world values.

He demands that I love my neighbor—my orphan neighbor, my starving neighbor, my imprisoned neighbor, my living-off-the-system neighbor—as much as I love myself.

I want this, I do, but there are still days I try hard to convince myself I've let go of enough, that I've met my quota. When it comes to living a long life well, I don't think our hearts mean any harm. We all just want to feel something. That's why we overeat, overspend, overcommit. We're numbed by our antiseptic standard of what a "good life" requires, so we squeeze its limits hoping to feel—respected, envied, cool, capable, smart, proud. It doesn't really matter; we're just so tired of the status quo. We're tired of this crushing restlessness. Our bones and our souls ache with wanting, but our remedies are all wrong.

I do well to remind myself we're still among the wealthiest

people in the world. Here I still sit, in my comfortable, safe home with uneaten food in the trash. It's hard to stomach some days. It's hard to justify one more lackluster sweater or an immersion blender. But not hard enough that I don't do it all the time. I keep looking, but I simply cannot find the red-letter words I need to support my cause of having more. I want to believe it's someone else's turn to sacrifice. But the truth rings clear. I still have a choice. Every day. My calling doesn't change.

Over the past year, Cory and I have lost enough sleep over this "How much is enough?" question to rejuvenate an entire MOPS (Mothers of Preschoolers) group of sleep-deprived mamas.

Unfortunately—or fortunately, depending on the day—there's no magic number or safe zone. What this means is, we're required to keep our ears pressed against the Holy Spirit if we want to walk in his way. All we need is his daily bread, his precise "enough" for each of our unique lives. What would happen if more of us built the roof at that level of "enough"? Everything above that amount isn't ours to hold on to. Everything above it goes back to the source—to help alleviate some of the pain around us and prosper his kingdom.

Our friend Jon has been asking the same question. Working with Tiny Hands International, an organization committed to fighting human trafficking in South Asia, he has a front-row seat to the restoration of some of our world's most abandoned people. More than once, Jon has mused that maybe the goal should be to live off 10 percent and let God keep what's already his. Admittedly, he's not there yet, and we're not even close. But it's an interesting idea, this flipping of our evangelical tithing paradigm.

We've tied the Old Testament idea of tithing like a noose around the gospel commandment to give sacrificially. We applaud the widow and her two coins (Mark 12:41–44) with secret relief that we're not her. There's plenty left over after we shave off our Christian surcharge and toss it in the plate. I don't know what made me believe I'm not her. I'm not sure how I convinced myself our situations were so different. She gave all she had. She lived as though it wasn't hers in the first place and forked it over without a blink. Meanwhile, we split hairs over whether our tithe should be off our net or gross income. We haggle with God and walk away believing we've earned our blessing until the next payday.

Honestly, it's alarming.

When we believe we're entitled to keep 90 percent of whatever we earn, our capacity to truly care about the kingdom of God and his people—our neighbors—is kept at bay. It's stunted. To our own detriment.

I'm sick to death of trying to trick God into believing my heart is in the right place while I count my nickels and fear overpaying him.

Capping our lifestyle would totally take the pressure off. Think of the hours and years we could save if we didn't have to waste another minute trying to wrestle our way into something bigger, better, nicer, if we knew to our core we already had exactly enough.

A shift like this could have a sweeping impact on global poverty, local lack, and especially the cultural rift between the church and a world that has lost the will to connect with her. More than anything, I believe the biggest change would happen in the chambers of my own greedy heart. Despite how much things have already changed, it is still ridiculously hard for me to part with my cash.

Never mind the big idea of only living with what we need.

I've seen what "need" looks like, and even if I dramatically sheared excess from my life, I would still fall easily on the side of comfort and that pesky "I want it" mentality.

"Need" is not something I'm quite ready to tackle. If you've spent any length of time in a third-world country, you might understand my reluctance. We are a people so steeped in what we want that we can't imagine life without our tchotchkes and face serums and throw pillows and entire refrigerator drawers full of organic vegetables and fancy yogurt. Some of us (cough, cough) have seasonal bed linens and rotatable wall art. I understand minimalism is the new black; I'm just not ready to wear it.

Still. Let's be quasi-reasonable, people. Let's at least try.

I don't have all the answers on what "enough" is. I don't even have the answers for my own family. Our ear is pressed against the Father, he's leading us, and it continues to feel like freedom. Until we find our exact "enough," we're learning to recognize ever-deepening layers of "too much." Too much is the thing that is not on the table.

It's the house we would never, ever sell. It's the overpriced jeans that we won't give up because they're the only ones that fit right, or the boots that all the cool women on Instagram are wearing when last year's are fine. Too much is the eight-hundred-dollar farm table we could buy with cash but not without leaving a pit in our stomachs. Too much is four boxes of on-sale strawberries when we know we won't eat more than three before they go bad.

Too much is that thing we justify. The lifestyle that dictates our career path. It's whatever our fingers are clenched around. It's what we think we deserve or have earned.

I see excess in my life every day. I may not always choose to respond in obedience, but I have asked God to show me my "too much," and he has followed through.

We have miles and miles to go, and financial stewardship is a constant battle. I love cute outfits, old junk, and Gorgonzola cheese. None of those things are bad, especially not the cheese, but all of them theoretically *could* be bad.

Jesus calls us to live, move, and love in reverse. It's never the way we thought it would be. It's not what we would have scripted if the pen were in our hands.

That's what kingdom living is. It's about holding loosely. It's about believing—really believing—that I'll be held accountable for all of it one day. I can't answer for you or for him, but I'd better be ready to answer for Shannan Martin.

4

UNPLAN

A life surrendered to the Spirit of God is a life lived with open hands, palms turned upward in letting go. We have to let go so we can live.

—*EVERY LITTLE THING*, DEIDRA RIGGS[1]

IT HAPPENED ON the fly, the second time Robert moved back home from jail.

We'd been down this road before, just one year earlier, but after eight months with us, he'd moved out on his own, only to wind up right back where he started.

Round two was queuing up before our eyes. And for all the ways each of us had shifted, recalibrated, and done our best to coexist peacefully the first time around, we couldn't plead ignorance this time. We all knew what we were getting ourselves into, and it looked something like the angst of two very different worlds colliding. It looked like rap music, slamming doors, YouTube marathons, and so much love.

Of course we said yes when he shouted across the phone line

from his factory job, "Mom, I reached the highest level at Work Release. Can I come home for the rest of my home detention?"

"Can I come home . . . ?" The kid is flawless when it comes to negotiating the best possible outcome for himself. Brilliant word choice, son. Brilliant!

As thrilled as we were to have another six-month shot at sharing a roof and loving him well, a small part of us teetered. This wasn't our idea. It wasn't what we had planned. I'll state the obvious: *we still didn't get it.* And I'm beginning to wonder whether we ever will. I'm beginning to see an unfortunate pattern in myself, in which I view sacrifice as situational. Temporary.

Sure, we can do hard things, but only if we have time to emotionally prepare, only if we have the option of doing said hard thing on *our* terms. Robert moving in a second time had never, ever been discussed. This idea was decidedly not on our terms. I was supposed to be writing a book, after all. I require bulk doses of peace and quiet when I write, and Robert has the volume level of an entire kindergarten class combined with the physical presence of a moody, fire-breathing circus acrobat. Had God never met me and my particular needs? Did he have no respect at all for timing?

Love won the internal clash. The battle was brief and without bloodshed. We braced ourselves, and he blew back through our door, all six feet four of him, with his ankle bracelet, his smokes, his twenty-one years of collected habits and quirks, and his relentless optimism. It was the best sort of sucker punch.

The littles displayed the giddy relief of schoolkids on a snow day that he was home again, and the needle on our chaos meter climbed. Though God still had some explaining to do, we were stouthearted in our willingness to make it all work despite the interruptions to our life and our precious plans. We could totally rally.

Two days later we got a call asking if we would be willing to unofficially foster a two-and-a-half-year-old little girl named Gracie. Suddenly, having Robert at home seemed like child's play.

Here's a brief summary of what happened after that call:

- A rapid-fire phone conversation with Cory, in which we both stood slack-jawed and speechless until one of us finally said, "I think we should do it," and the other followed with, "Me too."
- A hasty, uncomfortable meeting in our living room with all relevant parties.
- A quick calculation on available sleeping quarters, which led to . . .
- The inspired conclusion that we were underresourced in square footage, prompting . . .
- The decision to bunk the two girls together, which first required . . .
- Moving Cory and me downstairs into the toy room, which desperately needed . . .
- A fresh coat of paint, which meant . . .
- Moving all the ~~junk~~ important educational implements elsewhere.

Having been solidly and safely past parenting toddlers for several years, we now needed to procure such throwback novelties as a crib, tiny shirts, tiny forks, tiny socks, tiny toys, tiny *everything*. And diapers.

There would be meetings with an attorney, doctors' offices, and day cares.

We were on the line for roughly forty-seven signatures and enough text messages between Gracie's mom, Gracie's grammy, and us to travel the Northwest Passage twice.

Oh, and we had two days to do it.

You get my drift. This was the can't-catch-our-breath, what-just-happened, not-on-our-list inconvenience of the modern age. Times two.

Funny thing was, we thought we had already been there, done that.

When Cory and I both lost our lucrative jobs within a couple of months of each other, just a month after bringing home our heartbroken Siley, we felt the ground rumble beneath our feet. It seemed the earth might cleave at any moment, and while we knew we'd land on the same side of the chasm, we were terrified of what we would lose in the process.

The years that followed felt like the Viking ship ride at King's Island, where the bow swings up, then the weight shifts to the stern, over and over, with increasing momentum until you almost puke.

Back and forth. We would adjust to world-rocking change just in time for the next wave to hit.

There were job transitions, unexpected financial crises, and Haven in the upstairs guest room.

And then there was our move to the city, which is a whole other story.

We were pretty confident we had reached our quota on doing difficult things after all that.

Yet there we were, two weeks after our foster daughter arrived, stuck inside during a blizzard like sardines in their tin, a cobbled-together family of seven, not sharing a strand of DNA among us.

Incidentally, I'm not awesome at being snowed in with seven people in a smallish house. Seven. People. One in diapers. Several who are extroverts. The tallest and the two shortest who *never stop talking.*

Our once-tranquil life was disrupted a few years back, and there still seems to be no end to the aftershocks. Where we were once cute, quiet, and quaint, we are now loud, messy, scattered, and occasionally (daily) tense. My type-A personality has downgraded to a solid Q. I've hoisted the white flag on things that used to really matter to me, like balanced meals, tidy surfaces, and, now and then, basic hygiene.

It all makes perfect sense.

Because if there's one thing I've learned, it's that God gets a massive kick out of flinging his people into chaos. The Bible is riddled with examples of the way he moves among us, and I hate to be the one to break it to you, but he rarely comes off looking like a gentle dove. Loving? Yes. Always. But we're talking about the God who launched constellations and galaxies into the far reaches of a universe he designed, the one who craved a human race of children created in his image, then allowed an inborn nature of selfishness, greed, and fear. Our God is a fist-pumping, raucous-laughing, barn burner of a dad. He's a total rabble-rouser. His economy is often not rich with productivity or a visible long-range strategy. He almost never makes sense to folks like you and me.

He chooses discomfort, challenges common sense, and promises pain in exchange for our very lives and all they harbor— our dollars, our hours, our homes, our families, our closely held dreams of a rosy future.

This is the God we say we love. This is the God we signed up for. He kept nothing from us, made no false claims, hid zero agendas, and we said *yes*. We said we wanted the life he had to offer, and that we would follow wherever he led in order to find it.

And yet we often feel all baited-and-switched when those dusty roads don't lead us back to ourselves as planned.

When this feeling of holy trickery rains down on me, the inevitable question is, shouldn't I know him better than this? One of my earliest memories is sucking on the pew in front of me during church. Born into a family with a Bible-to-human ratio of roughly 4:1, God has been a constant presence in my life.

This was my very history, the faith of my grandpas and parents, Zacchaeus, Georges Washington *and* Bush, Queen Esther, Amy Grant, and, reportedly, Michael Sever. It was tradition and truth, handed down, handed down, landing square in my lap.

I knew all about the wacky faith of Noah, who built an ark apart from the context of rain, much less a flood. I remembered young David with his five smooth stones and Daniel, who lounged with lions. I memorized the stories, but their brand of faith seemed foreign to my own. God used to be crazy, but he'd settled down over the course of . . . forever. This is the twenty-first century and, God only knows, none of us has time for that vintage, Old Testament nonsense.

He used to light up bushes, part seas, and infest entire nations with frogs. He birthed babies in the elderly, had a fish swallow a grown man, and told Abraham to tie his son to an altar.

Yet when it came to me, when all he asked was for me to pound a For Sale sign into my front yard and find his people, it was way too much. Crazy talk. It was so utterly beyond the bounds of my reality, I believed I was hearing him wrong.

My job, I believed, was to advance my agenda, as long as it was God's will. And of course it was God's will. My game plan didn't just resemble the ideals I was surrounded with; it mirrored them. From my birth until well into my thirties, I processed and cataloged the cues of my Christian brethren without ever stopping to consider the ways our collective uniformity might pose a threat to each of us.

We all wanted the same things. We all loved Jesus. We were good to go. Right?

With knocking knees, I stood between everything I'd ever known and the God who scripted me into being. He had things for me to do. He stood ready to blow my plans out of the water, if I'd let him.

I wish I could say the choice was easy, that following God amid uncertainty was a complete no-brainer.

It wasn't easy. It was painful. Wrenching. Confusing. Unclear. There were times it felt like the flu and a long string of days that ended with my face pressed against a soggy pillow.

Because of his fierce love for me, and his unflinching knowledge that what he offered was so much better than the ghetto of my scared, secluded faith, he nudged and needled and shoved me around.

Until, finally, I jumped.

Upside-Down and Backward

Here's what I know now. I know God calls us. To do actual things that are often way out of bounds in the eyes of the world and even the church.

For most of my life, I had attended church, sung like I meant it, tithed, and made the near-fatal mistake of molding Scripture around my plans for my future. I started young.

I'll paint you a little picture. When I was fifteen, I fell head-long into the high school crush of the ages, giddy and distracted, fully unprepared for the emotional fallout circling overhead like Poe's raven of doom.

A couple of months later, *Crush of the Ages Part Two* descended, taking up as much adolescent emotional real estate as the first. My guts were getting crowded, and my friends were already sick to death of hearing about it.

You can't imagine the torment.

For upwards of a year I dutifully sat on my polka-dot comforter each night before bed with a package of loose-leaf notebook paper and penned nearly identical longhand pleas to God, asking him to resolve my confusion and bring about his perfect will for my life.

It was either the church boy or the boy down the road. I gave God two options. The suspense nearly inverted my psyche.

I had never felt closer to God.

Night after night I made him exactly who I needed him to be. I asked the same questions and drew identical conclusions. I underlined, memorized, copied, and recopied what had quickly become my favorite Bible verse: "Trust in the LORD with all your heart and lean not on your own understanding; in all

your ways submit to him, and he will make your paths straight"
(Prov. 3:5–6 NIV).

Since it was carved permanently into my temporal lobe from
sheer overuse, paraphrasing wasn't necessary. Still, I lived and
moved and passed triangular notes to my friends in a state of
metaphysical paraphrase. It was the backbeat for all the hours I
couldn't actively obsess to God or my long-suffering friend, Sarah.

> *I trust you, Lord, to eventually tell me definitively
> which of these two cute boys will take my hand in marriage
> in roughly seven to ten years. Though it seems neither guy has
> any interest in me, I choose to transcend my human under-
> standing and submit to your obvious will, believing you will
> bring a hasty resolution to this problem, particularly since
> both are headed away to college soon and time's a-wasting
> (hint, hint), amen.*

I jimmied the flawless Word of God into a means to *my* end.

I desperately wish I could say this was my sole instance of
gross misconduct with Proverbs 3:5–6. I wish I could chalk it all
up to the same sort of teenaged insecurity and self-involvement
that prompted me to pad my bra that one time or try out for the
cheerleading squad when I possessed all the limb-control of an
infant giraffe.

In fact, I misinterpreted and misapplied those verses and
others like it (I'm looking at you, Jeremiah 29:11!) so often, I
truly believed what I was doing was right. This proof-texting
largely formed the foundation of my faith.

Over and over I hatched a plan and said it was God's, retro-
actively mining the Bible for any truth—context optional and

perhaps even undesirable—on which I could hang my shaky, me-centric conclusions.

I clung to verses like James 1:6 (NIV), "But when you ask, you must believe and not doubt," underlining them until the page nearly wore through, doing my best to avoid passages like those just one page over:

> Look here, you who say, "Today or tomorrow we are going to a certain town and will stay there a year. We will do business there and make a profit." How do you know what your life will be like tomorrow? Your life is like the morning fog—it's here a little while, then it's gone. What you ought to say is, "If the Lord wants us to, we will live and do this or that." Otherwise, you are boasting about your own pretentious plans, and all such boasting is evil. (James 4:13–16)

Who wanted to worry about life as fog and evil boasting? Not me. Didn't have time for it.

Having safely traversed the ills of my youth, the things I wanted as a legit adult were now "good" things, things like comfort, security, prosperity, and safety. I outlined a plan and assumed God was along for the ride, obligated in some way to bless the journey while I gripped the reins.

I turned the gospel upside-down, angling it to fit my needs, when all God wanted, in his infinite affection, was for *me* to be turned upside-down by *him*. For *his* purposes and plans. God was desperate to give me his best gifts, but in order to receive them, I had to let go of all the wrong things I was holding.

Upon reflection my grabby hands and I needed a stone-cold lesson in letting go.

Our Favorite Detour

It should go without saying that, often, letting go is not our idea. We're conditioned to receive, not to relinquish. God wants dominion over every area in my life. Even worse, he has made it clear he already has it. It is his. Always has been. Basically, I can lay it down willingly, or he'll wrestle me for it. But he wants what is his—namely, me.

He wants my heart and my soul. He wants to give me the desires of my heart but can't bear another day of watching me want everything but him. I say I belong to God, but our priorities often form a Venn diagram that barely overlaps. On paper, we are hardly related.

Letting go of control is a tremendous risk to my DIY faith and my white-knuckled existence. Control is my favorite illusion. My pet. A solace when the night rolls in. It keeps me company when the house is quiet and the halls are dark. It robs me of my appetite and creeps up on me like a cold sore. But there is a choice to be made, and it requires choosing myself or God.

Can I really trust enough to believe my plans are meaningless apart from him, the one who sees all, knows all, created everything down to the annoying birthmark by my left eye?

I want to believe I do trust like that, but I start thinking of heartbreaking and terrifying things, like dying and spending my life submerged in the mess of reality, and the temptation is to just shut it all down. Given the choice, I always detour around discomfort. I prefer my life pretty. And simple. I don't want to go there, because it's too complicated. It gives me the blues.

Our culture bombards us with the message that we should aspire to have more and do less. Slow is the new salsa. We're reminded constantly to make time for ourselves, and if I hear the oxygen mask analogy one more time (save yourself first!), I might poke shish kebab skewers into my ears. *Say no! Stay home!* This is what we're told to do when we're not being shouted at about where to shop and what to drive, and you know you need the newest iPhone, and by the way, you're wearing last year's plaid.

I gobble all of it up.

Staying home is perhaps the greatest luxury I know, roundly beneficial to everyone's wellness, and I'm even getting better at saying no to some things. These messages aren't wicked lies, and I'll be honest: a few weeks ago I succumbed to an updated plaid shirt. I just find myself wondering if the "me first" messaging is even necessary. It doesn't strike me as something we need help with, this prioritizing of ourselves. And then there's the wee problem that it runs contrary to the gospel.

God offers a better way: have less and do more. He inverts our plans, extending the option of total surrender like a May bouquet of decadent, gutsy, full-bloom peonies. It's not some dreary prison sentence, meant for the poor souls commissioned to overseas ministry, or monks or nuns. It's a hold-on-to-your-hat promise that life is actually far too long to risk squandering it on the wrong things. We're offered the gift of becoming laser-focused on doing more for his kingdom.

We get to exhaust our reserves because it matters. We get to say yes. We are allowed to grow passionate about justice, dream big, and live boldly. It's going to be all right. I promise. God gives us the Sabbath and commands us to take it. In the meantime, we might as well reroute our regularly scheduled lives.

Luke 5 is a full-color picture of what it looks like to walk toward right things. In it, Jesus was going about his business, preaching good news to the crowds pressing in around him. He noticed an empty boat up near the shore and asked its owner, Simon, if he could borrow it for a sec. Jesus was boxed in. The crowd was too large. He needed some distance in order to be seen, and the only place to go was out to sea.

Simon agreed. It had been one of those days. His nets were empty, and he was ready to pack it in and head home. Basically, he had nothing to lose. The finicky sea had already put a snag in his agenda.

After Jesus finished speaking, he told Simon to row farther out, let down his nets, and catch some fish.

"'Master,' Simon replied, 'we worked hard all last night and didn't catch a thing. But if you say so, I'll let the nets down again'" (v. 5).

"But if you say so, I'll let the nets down again."

Simon defied all logic and kicked common sense in the teeth. He risked his reputation and surrendered his time. Remember, this man was an expert in his field. He knew when to cast his nets and when to call it a day. Yet he was willing to throw out all his knowledge and years of experience simply because Jesus said so.

And that's not even the most amazing part. It gets so much better.

Simon let down the nets, and they filled with fish. There were so many fish, he had to scream for his buddies, James and John, to bring their boat for the overflow. The nets were now shredded, and the boats were both on the verge of sinking. This was the catch of a lifetime. It was more than he could have ever imagined or dreamed.

If he were a teacher, it would be like all his students whistling as they aced the government-standardized testing. If he were a chef, it would be a three-star Michelin review and a packed reservation book. If he were a writer, it would be like reaching eight thousand words in one day, and liking all of them.

Their plans were officially obliterated, in the best possible way.

I imagine Jesus with his mouth wide open as he laughed along with them and all those fish. This was their livelihood. Their currency. They were essentially loaded. Jesus provided exactly what they wanted. Of course it was a miracle, but how on earth were they going to get all those fish home?

Jesus' response? "Don't be afraid! From now on you'll be fishing for people!" (v. 10).

I can only imagine those tired, filthy, fishy-smelling, bewildered, bearded men had no clue what he was talking about. It didn't matter. Want to know what they did?

They sailed back to shore, "left everything," and "followed Jesus" (v. 11).

They let go.

They believed life was too long to spend it on their old ideas, so they jumped off the safe-track to success, believing it was the only way to freedom.

They weren't the only ones.

James and John left their boat and their dad. Matthew ditched his profession as a tax collector—then hosted a banquet for Jesus and the "scum" with whom he used to work. Just one encounter with their wrecking-ball Savior, and each man abandoned the very things that had once defined them.

Think of your life now. Think of what you hold most tightly. What could reflexively cause you to open your hands?

When it was time for us to let go of our farm, people came

in from all sides saying our home was a gift from God. He had made a way for us to have our hearts' desire. Through the strangest turn of events, we were handed the deed and the keys and moved into our dream. Almost no one understood why we would drop that net full of fish and walk away.

Why would he ask for it back?

Honestly, there was a time we wondered the same thing.

One encounter with God's sovereign love and consuming power can change your heart's desires on a dime, and I don't mind taking the liberty to say that if Simon were sitting next to me right now, he'd be nodding in agreement. It doesn't mean it will be easy or simple or that there won't be some mid-grade anxiety. There's a difference between being too scared to do hard things and doing hard things scared. Communing with the God of the universe will inspire all kinds of unscripted movement and giant leaps past "normal." It'll make surrendering seem like the safest way.

The Cost of Our Plans

In John 1, Nathaniel proclaimed Jesus the Son of God based solely on the evidence that Jesus said he saw him standing under a fig tree. Homeboy was just looking for a reason to believe. "You saw me under the fig tree? *I was under the fig tree!* Let me drop my entire life so I can walk beside you, Jesus." It had to have cracked Jesus up in the very best way. This is classic child-like faith, the kind he wants from you and me.

If you're a mom or a teacher or an aunt or any human who has ever experienced the wonder of a child, you get this. My youngest still thinks I'm a genius for the way I tie his shoes in an even double-knot, and my daughter once gushed about how much I must love her after I "made" ramen noodles for lunch.

Every time this sort of thing happens, I feel the heart-pinching goodness Jesus must have felt when he responded, "Do you believe this just because I told you I had seen you under the fig tree? You will see greater things than this" (v. 50).

In other words, "Dude, if you thought that was impressive, you'd better go ahead and tighten up those sandal straps."

Our simple human brains just can't fathom his goodness, or the way it sometimes orients itself as a hot mess. As written in Isaiah 43:18–19:

> But forget all that—
>> it is nothing compared to what I am going to do.
> For I am about to do something new.
>> See, I have already begun! Do you not see it?
> I will make a pathway through the wilderness.
> I will create rivers in the dry wasteland.

We know God often sends us to unfamiliar places to do difficult things, but he promises his yoke is easy and his burden light. He tells us point-blank that he'll lead us into the wilderness and wastelands, but he'll cut a path for us. He'll make rivers where there should only be drought.

In our case, his yoke is a lower income and friends living in poverty, racked with addictions. Our wilderness is a neighborhood where people tack airbrushed wolf blankets over their windows because they're suspicious of the light. Our wasteland is a low-income public school that keeps changing our lives for the better.

Forget all those things you saw him do before, back when you thought the path to life meant getting and gaining and striving and protecting. That's nothing compared to what he's going to do now that you have seen his off-kilter kingdom with fresh eyes.

I so desperately want to be an "if you say so" follower, like Simon, rather than an "if it's convenient and seems like a good idea" church lady.

I want to be captivated. Awestruck. Gobsmacked. Filled with the wonder of the living God. I want to hold so loosely to my life, my plans, and my long-held beliefs that they can all be boxed up in minutes, freeing me to follow wherever Jesus leads.

I'm sick to death of trudging through life using "life's too short" as my excuse to numb myself with things that eventually leave me wanting.

We complicate everything with our analytical, control-freak, ducks-in-a-row way of "searching" for God's will. He's not about playing games. He might not always show us the big picture, but his baby steps leave little room for confusion.

In the case of Philip, "an angel of the Lord said to him, 'Go south down the desert road that runs from Jerusalem to Gaza.' . . . The Holy Spirit said to Philip, 'Go over and walk along beside the carriage'" (Acts 8:26, 29).

Go south, Philip. Go walk beside the carriage.

Sell your house, Martins.

Become a mom and a dad to that man-child over in the county jail.

Move your bed to the toy room, and find a crib.

Your life will never be the same.

My God loves me. He wants to own my identity and boss

my schedule around. Yep. He wants to keep cramming people into this smallish house and into my heart. He wants my days to feel so unmanageable that I impulsively turn my back to the room while I'm stirring marinara and say, out loud, "Jesus, take the wheel," without an iota of Carrie Underwood irony.

God wants me at the end of myself so he can build me back up in ways that reflect more goodness, more him. He wants my self-pity and ego to be sacrificed on the altar of Much Better Things.

When we know the one who ordained the seasons and the wingspan of a singular burnished oak; who invented sugar and salt and the perfect sphere of a hardy cherry tomato; who knew how comforted we would be by things like wool and tea and the light in our babies' eyes; when we *know him*, we know that all his schemes, even the seemingly nutso ones, are for our gain. And when we trust that, when we really believe it, our fingers start to loosen their grip, and we reach out to touch the very edges of freedom.

That's what letting go is, after all. It's freedom.

🍃 🍂 🍃

Suffice it to say, my family narrowly survived the Snowpocalypse, cementing a specific bond that occurs when people triumph together over catastrophe. The winter was as brutal as our home was loud, a blaring parade of months with a record number of school cancellations and more than one morning where the news came in before dawn and I cried quiet, salty tears onto my pillow before rallying to make pancakes. Again.

When I tell you we were cooped up and antsy, I need you

to picture an actual coop, full of hormonal chickens. We coped in different ways. I baked carby things on the regular. The kids tore the upstairs apart and erected a mammoth fort that remained intact for weeks. Cory grew a most ridiculous beard (the worst rebellion?), and Robert sucked down menthols on the front porch, "quitting" every week or so, just until he was able to procure a fresh pack.

Eventually spring breezed in to town and when the snow was cleared away, we weren't surprised at all to find ourselves still standing. Together. Surveying the landscape, I found myself asking, "What would it have cost me if all my plans had panned out?" My answer was a no-brainer: it would have cost me every bit of this.

So you might have your family. You might have a job, a hobby, and a home that you love. You might think that all the big items have been checked off the list and you're mostly settled into a groove, *done*.

But maybe there's more. Maybe there's something over in the west or off to the east a little.

Wherever it is, let's trust the sender.

Let's *go*.

5

LIVE SMALL

Jesus is often in the last place I want to look but the very place he always said he would be—in the whisper, in the children, in the small and secret places.

—*Simply Tuesday*, Emily P. Freeman[1]

A YEAR AFTER our move to the city, it had become obvious that we would, indeed, be fine. For all the exaggerated talk of drug dealers and gang lords, this new land was surprisingly thick with hipsters and Mennonites.

In fact, we were more than fine. We were thriving. It may not have looked like that to our friends, given the fact that we had less money, less house, and more drama in our life, but it's certainly how it felt. We'd fallen in love with our city and our neighborhood. Making up for several decades of wasted time, we were busy leaning into the people around us and letting them teach us about diversity, acceptance, and the profound miracle of listening. The work was hard sometimes, but the work was working. At last, after realizing we truly weren't our own best interest, life was colored with meaning.

Rolling down a forgotten side street in my sexy minivan on an ordinary spring Thursday, I felt the air shifting once again. I wedged the phone tighter against my shoulder and shushed the frenzied wildlife buckled neatly behind me in three ratty booster seats.

There were new decisions to be made, and try though we did, Cory and I had failed for ten straight nights to nail them down from the comfort of our newish home. Maybe a phone call in the jangly van was just the shift in perspective we needed to gain some clarity, but the stakes of this discussion seemed too big for our chaos-on-wheels.

Up to that point in our marriage, Cory had been a real suit-and-tie kind of guy. Though his intelligence and drive were never secrets to me, I can't say I ever expected him to rub shoulders with the president—only twice, but still—or hobnob with the kind of people who have their names carved onto the sides of buildings and hire Lionel Richie for their daughter's wedding reception. Cory's former career didn't even make sense in hindsight, especially considering the current state of my ride.

But things were changing. Though his position at the alternative school was going smoothly, there was an unexpected job offer on the table. Neither of us saw this one coming.

The wind whipped my hair while Cory, a seasoned veteran of ten straight days of obsessing, ticked off the pros. Aside from the most obvious perk—the opportunity to speak truth into the lives of marginalized men—there were other practical perks. The hours would be more compatible with, well, *life*. His suits and ties could be pushed permanently to the back of the closet. He could finally grow a beard.

We drew sharp breaths, stockpiling our reserves for the cons.

Strangely enough it wasn't losing another third of his salary that slashed his resolve at the knees.

"I can't stop thinking that if I make this move, I might never regain my footing. I might lose my connections. It would be a permanent step backward," he said.

Instinctively a response tumbled from my mouth. "Every turn we've taken lately has been a step backward."

And there it was, the truth neither of us had wanted to hear. The one that freed us to continue on the under-arc of reason.

He laughed, because I was right. Then he went ahead and became the blue-jeaned, bearded chaplain of the county jail.

Smallness Is a Choice

Here's a reality check: we take up precious little square footage in the scope of God's great kingdom. Of all the facets of our faith, this might be one of the more difficult to grasp. It's also one of the most central.

We know somewhere up in our heads that the whole point of life is to reflect God's glory by becoming more like his Son. The how-to manual is right in front of us. But honestly, we're just not that into what it has to say about our stature in this world. The Jesus way of humility doesn't align with our self-made gospel of achievement, and we're willing to sell our souls at the corner of trying to have both.

What if, instead, we simply let go? That's the unfancy gospel we're called to, to open our hands and fall; to cultivate a deep love for low places; to stop elevating ourselves as anything other than poor and needy.

Philippians 2:5–8 says:

> You must have the same attitude that Christ Jesus had. Though he was God, he did not think of equality with God as something to cling to. Instead, he gave up his divine privileges; he took the humble position of a slave and was born as a human being. When he appeared in human form, he humbled himself in obedience to God and died a criminal's death on a cross.

Jesus shed heaven and descended into the muck of earth, where all its inhabitants were jockeying for more clout, more esteem, more money, more power, more respect, more, more, more. He walked away from perfection in order to be a friend and neighbor to damaged goods.

Paul says Jesus took the position of a slave "and was born as a human being." It's worded as though it was a remarkable choice, *because it was*. By leaving the physical presence of God, walking away from absolute holiness and a sweeping absence of darkness in order to move "into the neighborhood" (John 1:14, THE MESSAGE) of soul-poverty and hearts that had lost their way, his intentions were clear. He didn't cop to our "smart" standards of behavior. He didn't stick to the script when it came to social strata, class systems, and acclaim. He essentially showed up and demolished our regime.

That he came to be with us when he could have kept his post at the right hand of God should send us running breathless into every busted-up city, every barred-up shack, every cave, every cell, every pain-drenched street corner we can find in order to bring the good news.

Instead we react exactly as expected, threatened by his choices and defensive over the way they cast shadows on our own. We want an out so dang bad. The company he kept and the way he valued nothing but relationships and eternity have us scrambling for an excuse to keep zipping through life with our shades on.

Christ chucked his status in order to walk with the forsaken, and I can't be bothered to invite them over for a cookout.

Imagine the lowest social position possible today. My mind goes to a homeless woman, addicted to meth, estranged from her children and parents, abused, easy, and uneducated, with broken teeth and a face full of shaky tattoos bartered from the guy in apartment 2B. This person I'm conjuring up certainly exists, and she lives somewhere within a twenty-mile radius of where you're sitting right now. I promise. Her life is uncomprehendingly difficult. She's judged and demoralized from every side, not given the time of day, never respected. We speak slowly to her, if we speak at all. We don't owe her eye contact or anything else. Maybe we pity her. Maybe we feel a hollow pang of guilt. But *she chose this mess she's in*, we say. *She made her bed.*

Jesus chose to show up on our lowest rung of social hierarchy as a squirming babe, painting a clear picture of his subversive take on status. An equivalent for us might be to scrap our airbrushed lives in order to take on the life of the woman we just imagined, then live it with her. He came in the form of us, living a life similar to ours, but he also came to live *with* us.

This central act of with-ness set the stage for the incarnation of Christ—you and me wearing his love like a shawl, sacrificing

our own comfort to lay it warm against another. This is no accident, and we've got to pay attention.

Embracing our smallness is the skeleton key for living the
abundant life.

This is the hope we've been given.

Living small is not about having less, but being less—less
respected in the eyes of the world, less successful, less wealthy,
less esteemed, less you. Less me. And more Jesus. Here, in
this abundance of less, where more of us is stripped away, we'll
uncover the person we were made to be, the one created in the
image of a God who sank holy feet into our human mess.

Jesus picked the short guy, the odd guy, the old guy, the sin-
prone guy. He picked the seductress, the simple, the sick.

Your son is dying? Lower him down.

You want to see me? Climb down.

You say you love me? Fall down.

Weak is strong, small is big, and less has most definitely
always been more.

Go ahead and sigh, because it turns out we weren't made for
world domination or national notoriety.

We are small. We were not made for greatness, and our
positioning inside the framework of forever is sort of irrelevant.

The God of the universe, the only one who can break our
chains, is calling us down.

Skinny

I've always found it endearing that God, in his infinite wisdom,
used a guy with a stutter to help deliver the Israelites and made
an adulterer with a felony record into a king. At some of my

lowest points, theirs were the stories I clung to, the idea that God could use weakness to redeem failure.

What I didn't realize was that these aren't the exceptions. They're simply a couple of the most popular examples of his standard operating procedure. Moses and David weren't meant to soothe us on our worst days but to be a mirror for us. Every single day.

The Bible is a collection of unlikely people used to magnify God's goodness and power. Stories of smallness aren't simply *in* the Bible; they *are* the Bible. It's stacked with imagery about children and mustard seeds, remnants and narrow gates, sparrows and lambs, a boy who defeated a giant, and a tiny infant redeemer.

In this manual for living, humility is the favored tool. To touch the expansiveness of God, we've got to befriend the ways we come up short. Our communion and the health of our community depend on our ability to see ourselves in condemned Rahab, abandoned Joseph, and worn-out, wary Sarah.

Growing up, I was always the runty, sickly kid. I kind of remember it, in that hazy way childhood appears to a middle-ager—ghostlike, gauzy.

What I can say for sure is that I've always been inexplicably scrawny. Year after year, doctors would stare me down, squint at my chart, then have me tested for type 2 diabetes. Or scoliosis. Or digestive issues. Or obscure genetic diseases. My immune system wasn't exactly exemplary, but there wasn't technically anything wrong with me. Even so, they persisted.

At the height of MTV's *We Are the World* campaign, a couple of my second-grade classmates identified me as a good replacement punch line for starvation jokes. (Have grace. We were busy trading scratch-and-sniff stickers and tucking our sweaters into our jeans. We didn't yet have a firm grip on third-world poverty or our place in its context, and our compassion was a work in progress.)

This string-bean pattern continued to startling effect, reaching its fever pitch in middle school, or as I remember it, the Dreaded Year of the Eights, when during the course of the eighth grade, I grew eight inches, graduated to a size eight-and-a-half shoe, and my eight-year-old sister could beat me up.

Needless to say, I have mixed feelings about being weak. On the one hand, weakness has always been an undeniable part of me. I couldn't change it if I tried. On the other hand, I've always seen it as a detriment and learned to creatively overcompensate.

While I'd never try to arm wrestle you, I learned how to throw down in a verbal spar. I became strong in other ways. I was the smart one. The mature one. The achieving one.

The first third of my life was devoted to proving my strength. *I don't need your help.*

But the truth is, weakness is a simple fact of life. It's what we all are, at our core.

We are weak. We need God, and we need his people. We need hope. We are but humans, in need of dark chocolate and a nap. We need strength to rise up and face our seven-year-old who still has strong urges and incomprehensible plans when it comes to household items such as soap, Band-Aids, rolls of tape, and any and all watertight containers. We need patience for the husband who "literally didn't notice" the laundry he stepped over to climb into bed. We need courage to walk fresh-picked blueberries across the street to the new neighbors who give us the side-eye, then shut the door a beat too quickly. (Maybe it's just me.)

What I'm beginning to see, though, is that God doesn't fix my weakness by making me strong. He becomes my strength in my perpetual weakness. He takes over. Constantly. He swoops in, ruffles my hair, and says not to worry, then charges to the top of the mountain I'm facing—the king of every hill I've ever stood upon with shaking knees. I am weak, and he is strong. He's all the strength I need, and my weakness doesn't have to flee in order for His presence to reign.

God is enchanted by my frailty.

It's why I need him.

It's why he showed up and never stops.

Irresponsible and Ordinary

A bedrock of my faith had always been the belief that obedience was rewarded. Follow Jesus—Go to heaven—with a million or so fantastic surprises in between. It's the ultimate benefits package, perfectly rounded, whole-life coverage representing various levels of reward (I'll take the "Platinum" reward package, please) including a larger celestial mansion and sparklier crown jewels.

When I read Paul's words, "Let's not get tired of doing what is good. At just the right time we will reap a harvest of blessing" (Gal. 6:9), I always assumed the "right time" was "pretty soon," like one to six months, max. I lived as though this temporary world were the big idea. I wanted to reap the best blessings *here*.

For years, I'd stood rail-straight in a world terrified of being typical. Lagging behind the curve was not an option. Somewhat subconsciously I believed God would make himself famous through my good reputation, my steadfast commitment, and my strict adherence to popular church culture. In a strange way

I believed God needed my greatness. I worked hard to prove myself worthy while torquing the gospel to bend around the *me* I was busy creating.

Since I'd made Olympic sport of deconstructing the Bible to fit my comfort level, where privilege is deserved and security is a hard-won goal, as my life progressed I modernized my definition of "blessing" to include only parameters of more—higher positioning, greater gain, elevated stature, and lauded reputation. If pressed, I'm sure I would have said it was all for God. I was doing my part to represent.

In terms of the Martins earning our place among the Church of the Sensible and Respected, we felt that our reputation was all ours. Hesitant as we may have been to admit it, our financial and other personal successes had involved at least a dash of luck or a bit of heavenly intervention. But our reputation? *That* was built on the proud backs of ourselves, everything else lining up snugly under its canopy. No one could take it away.

Except someone could, actually. And he did.

When large portions of our life began shifting, we were called irresponsible. Attention-seeking. Some said we were being prideful. People we barely knew—and some we'd never even met—trotted out accusations that we were being unsafe, even negligent.

I wouldn't say the words weren't felt. We can be strong, stouthearted people. We can hold our heads high and fake it while our feet shake in our suede ankle boots. But our skin was made thin. We aren't titanium-coated after all, so yes, sticks and stones do hurt, and words will also leave a mark. Want to know what I think? It's all part of the plan. We're small, remember?

We're no superheroes, especially not in the purview of eternity. We're children, and some days are sure to end with us crying our eyes out in our Father's lap.

I wish I had understood all of that while it was happening rather than in hindsight. At the time, I faked a strong front, but behind closed doors, I was shrinking into a self-protective cocoon, self-medicating with Santitas tortilla chips, unrecommended portions of salsa, and bad reality television.

It turns out, it's impossible to walk in the spirit of truth while running with the pack. My well-being and sanity depended on getting cozy with the fact that I was not here to please or impress anyone. People could talk if they wanted to, but the God who cleans up my messes does the same for all of us. I needed to be saved, not applauded.

So we surrendered our reputation, because it was a sham and it needed to go.

We began to see the profound beauty of setting the bar way down at the knees of our humanity, where we could unburden ourselves from the opinions of man while God did the heavy lifting of making his name great through his disaster-prone people, a grouping in which we finally found our home.

Our mistakes were no longer indictments intended for shame but opportunities to point to the redemption of the cross.

It totally took the pressure off.

❦ ❦ ❦

I have no idea why we're all so afraid of what people think of us. I only know we are.

We spend our entire lives propping ourselves up, angling our persona just so, contouring and shading, filtering and bedazzling in order to catch the brightest spot of light.

From there, one of two things happens. Either it doesn't work and we spin ourselves sick trying to fix the problem (exactly what *is* the problem?), or worse, people actually buy our hype and instead of gathering in the space of what's real, we spend our lives trying to stay above water on a sinking ship.

I won't speak for you, but here's an off-the-cuff list of attributes I hope spring to mind when you hear the words "Shannan Martin": smart, kind, responsible, funny, capable, generous, easy-going, blah blah blah. Would "captivating" be too much? "Iconic"? I'll settle for any of the descriptive words reserved for an Academy Award acceptance speech, or the eulogy of a beloved teacher or revered health care professional. That'll work just fine, thanks.

Here's my reality: I'm sitting here with yesterday's hair, on my unmade bed, with piles of laundry rising up around me and not calling me blessed. My day included a shouting match with one of my kiddos, followed by apologies, followed by round two. I started making something called Taco Pickles this morning before realizing I have four vinegars in the house, none of which is plain white vinegar, so I drove to the store for plain white vinegar and came home with a pineapple, a bag of Takis chips, two boxes of cereal . . . and no plain white vinegar. (Send help.)

Since that's not enough Shannan for you, I also forgot the birthday of one of my best friends, I haven't cracked open my Bible in several days, and I served lukewarm leftovers for dinner. And by "served," I mean I placed them on the island and walked away.

There was a day when I would have rather eaten soggy bread than tell the whole truth about myself.

But once God cracked my facade, I realized it's not our on-top-of-it-ness that connects us. It's our split-seamed, rusty-zippered baggage. On the quest to being more fully human, our faults and failures bring us down to where everyone else is pretending not to be.

Before long it's almost like a party here in the valley of humanity.

Last

We happen to be thick in the "me first" years of parenting here in the Martin household. I foolishly thought we had somehow managed to avoid them, but it turns out my kids are just late bloomers. A typical family with places to go and people to see, our shorties argue every single ding dang time we load up the van. Together, they've devised a convoluted protocol, wherein it's desirable to enter first, but equally desirable to be the first to exit. Of course, the two do not go hand in hand. I don't know everything about parenting, but I do know that if you get in first, you have to move your booty to the back row so everyone else can file in.

A few days ago, I noticed Ruby lagging behind when it was time to hop in and buckle up. She was glued to the sidewalk, not budging an inch, artfully dodging eye contact. Not that I'm prone to barking or anything (cough, cough), but this one time I did. "Get *in*!"

With the sincere innocence of a nine-year-old little girl, she said from her post on the sidewalk, "But you said the first should be last and the last one got to be first. So I'm making sure I'm really last so I can be first."

It's funny, because it's familiar.

Don't we all secretly feel that way? Aren't we angling for the hidden perks that must come with being first? Doesn't first mean best? I sure live as though it's true.

I thought becoming a doctor would sort of designate me as one of the "first," with all those extra initials tacked onto my name and the smart lab coat. When those plans fell apart in my first semester of college—long story, but the highlight reel includes my calculus professor hopping on top of his desk in a fit of rage when two-thirds of us flunked the first exam—I was left with no choice but to piece together a sturdy plan B. I'd have to angle myself as "best" and "first" in other ways. I had my work cut out for me. All I needed to do was raise the most agreeable children, have the cutest house, somehow achieve shampoo-commercial hair, and write a blog post that would go viral.

Do you need me to tell you how this story ended? Must I point to the books lining my shelf on how to "support" my "strong-willed child"? My kids have maintained a strong level of behavioral gusto. My cute home that "made" my blog is long gone. I still have lackluster hair now graying in patches. And not a word I've written has ever gone viral.

I've always been terrified of being somehow classified as last. I grew up believing the best I had to offer God and the world was my actual shiniest best. I never imagined my offering to the kingdom would start with a swift kick off the ladder. I was going to have to find a way to bear with my smallness, because it began to seem like the biggest part of me.

The sixth chapter of Mark describes Jesus as "just a carpenter."

I suppose he could have come in a flashier way, and his refusal to do so is telling. Of course, this doesn't mean we should question the intentions of everyone wearing a white collar or taking a stage. It simply means that we have been handed the gift of knowing for sure that our identity needn't hinge on what the world values.

God's plan for some is certainly to ace that first calculus test and eventually take the Hippocratic oath. But for others it could be to skip college and work at the plasma bank on the west side of town, where many of my friends and their friends show up regularly in order to make some cash and keep their precarious lives afloat. Maybe God knew from the foundations of the earth that you'd one day be a well-suited banker, or maybe he knew you'd best shepherd his lambs as the manager of the Dollar Tree in the janky strip mall.

Want to have your world rocked for a quick minute? Maybe the same is true of your kids. Maybe their part in his grand kingdom means a factory job or working the fryer, and you'll be called to celebrate that success.

In order to live an abundant life, we will lose before we gain. We will be last so he can be first, but no worries, he won't forget in the end. God promises us gifts of loss and less, and though we know all his promises are for our good, we resist them. Still, our eye creeps up to the top of the ladder.

I once heard a businessman make the case for driving a gleaming Cadillac Escalade as part of his ministry to God's good work. Having met some success (in its classic definition), he set out to enhance that reputation with a vehicle that would instantly demonstrate his esteem and abilities. An outspoken believer, he made the natural—but dead wrong—connection between earthly "success" and being attuned to God's will. It gets a bit muddy, but basically, if he wanted to represent God well, he needed to be seen as a pillar of his community. And the most efficient way to elevate himself was by owning the right symbol. *Just look at how God has blessed him.*

When we tie our view of God to our view of a fallen world, the result is neither holy nor relevant. The two weren't meant to intersect. They run on parallel tracks. God's brilliance is alive in this kingdom on earth, but not on our terms. The decision we're faced with is, simply, do we want to jump the rails?

Smudged

Not long ago, I had the opportunity to provide a job reference for a twentysomething mother of four with a pretty checkered past. It took me way off guard when the call came in from a popular discount store. I hadn't spoken to this friend in nearly a year. Our relationship had ended like so many others before— the grief of a hard life bearing down until something snaps and they disappear.

I know lots of people who have worked retail jobs. I personally clocked three summers in the shoe department of a large grocery store (oh, America!) and have had friends and relatives who have worked at places like McDonald's or other minimum-wage jobs. The difference is, my friends and I made the choice to do it. For *this* friend, it was a last resort. Her problems stretched far beyond the power of that polyester smock, but it seemed like a good place to start.

The voice on the other end of the line asked just two questions about this candidate for employment. We're talking the bare necessities. She didn't inquire about her greatest strength or even if she was open to working Sundays. *Is she honest? Would you recommend her for the job?*

When my response included an unintended dramatic pause, the HR rep stifled a laugh. I'm sure she'd been in the exact position many times before. She knew the drill.

It's not terribly cut-and-dried to put yourself on the line for other people, particularly when you've stood at close range and watched them wade through an unbearable life of poverty, the sort that shapes a person from the outside in. Their self-worth winds up mangled, and their ability to wish for anything gets poached. The concepts of maintaining hope and planning for the future belong to the middle class, and they'll tell you that themselves.

Sitting with my phone pressed to my ear, faced with realities on opposing poles, I wasn't sure what to do. Given the sum of everything I knew about her, *would* I recommend her for the job?

Of course I did.

♦ ◗ ◢

Back before I had kids and an IKEA sectional and the dumb age spot on the end of my nose, I cowrote official reports about the "War on Poverty" from a cubicle in Washington, DC.

But let me back up.

When Cory and I first arrived in the capital, I had several job interviews lined up for things I was at least somewhat qualified to do. The likeliest option was that I'd take an entry-level position as a staffer for a member of Congress. My résumé—and, more importantly my connections—would have allowed for that.

Not eager to rule out other options, I showed up at a

well-known conservative think tank for a long-shot interview that ended up playing out like a contestant screening for *Jeopardy!*

I fielded questions ranging from federal politics. (Him: "Who was the thirteenth president?" Me: "I don't know." Him: "Okay, who was the twenty-second?" Me: "I don't know."), to geography (Him: "If you were floating west down the Ganges River, where would you be headed?" Me: [stares blankly]), to literature (Him: "What is your favorite novel?" Me: [tries to think of the smartest-sounding novel I'd ever read, never mind the fact that I didn't even make it halfway through] *"Pride and Prejudice."* Him: "That's my wife's favorite novel!" Me: [silently pleads with God that I'm not asked a single follow-up question]).

I trust you get the point, though I could go on and on. For four hours. As in, when I arrived the office was bright and buzzing with smart people, and when I left the sky was black, and a wiry Midwestern girl was one step closer to infiltrating their ranks.

Though I proved no expert on history, math (he handed me a piece of scratch paper and a giant calculator), or basic trivia, when it came to what actually mattered, he summoned the faith of Abraham and believed I might have what it took. Two days later, I officially became the research assistant to one of the most prominent figures in America on welfare reform policy.

This beloved boss taught me the bones of writing, the discipline of thought, and the power of asking the right questions. We made a most unlikely duo.

Aside from the thrill of learning from him, the rest of the job description left me adrift, feeling like a misfit as I sat with colleagues in meetings, tapped the keys, and lunched in tucked-away cafés on Capitol Hill. The learning curve was steep; I was only an "expert" by association.

Still, I was "one of them," at least for a minute. We'd roll out the red carpets for members of Congress and government officials and feel so validated when they sipped our right-wing drinking water in their Brooks Brothers ties and seersucker suits. We told them about our solutions to American poverty, and the stats fell from our lips like air kisses. *Marriage is the greatest key to reducing child poverty. Recipients of government assistance should be required to work.*

More than ten years later, I can't argue with any of it.

In a perfect world every person would have access to gainful employment, and every baby mama would be a wife. The problem is, our world is fallen. The whole (air quotes) *poverty* issue isn't hypothetical or theoretical anymore. It can't be squashed with a mouthful of social science jargon.

Now, I know a woman whose wariness of the world coupled with her deepest desires to create stability and cobble together a makeshift family cost her her children. I know the roots of generational poverty coil up and around her family tree, taking on a positively viney appearance. She doesn't see the vines as a problem. She doesn't see them at all. They're part of her landscape, green-on-green, so all-encompassing and eternal as to be rendered invisible.

I know she sat in jail for half a year for a crime that wasn't hers, and I know every time I saw her there I felt the thrum of hopeful humanity reverberate from her to me through the tiny visitation monitor. I know she was too shy to ask for much, but when I pressed her, her request was a bra. She had already gone months without one.

Once freed, she continued to live in upheaval, chaos, and abuse. I know she has been hungry. I know she has almost given up.

Quick to expect people crushed by the stigma of poverty to replicate our lives, assuming our way is naturally best, we simply don't bother to do the hardest soul work of excavating the rest of the story. In a world where we know every outcome has a source, we isolate the bloom of need from the root of oppression.

God entrusted the poor to you and me, not to a ballot or a platform or a piece of whip-smart legislation.

He gave them to us because we're actual humans with lives, families, problems, and perspectives, in the unique position to learn their names, make them our own, and love them straight into the arms of their fixer. He waits to make us all "we" people, without delineations or tiers.

Having been the benefactor of a maverick risk-taker back in DC, I've experienced the power of being offered the opportunity to take on a job for which most would have (rightfully) said I was unqualified. My boss gave me a shot, risking his hard-won reputation on little old me, and though I'll always be grateful, the stakes were never insurmountable. There would have been other jobs. I haven't for a single day lived sequestered from opportunity.

Of course the disenfranchised around us need our kinship and encouragement, but even more they need our connections and our "good standing." In order to take seriously our job to fight against poverty, we have to acknowledge the gaps that exist between what the poor often have and what they desperately need. They need a future. They need hope and affirmation. They need to excavate their self-worth. They have Pop-Tarts and satellite TV. They have smartphones and shoes. But they can't get a job, and they make for risky tenants. Jon Katov, director of Open Table, said it well: "The poor need our intellectual and social capital. Not our used blue jeans and giant cans of Spaghettios."[2]

We send the poor our tired, worn-out stuff while we stay home with our clean hands and closed eyes, judging the way our government addresses a problem that was meant to be ours. We soothe ourselves with the idea that they need our sensibility or our "wisdom," but what they really need is for us to advocate for them, to hit the streets and sacrifice our reputation on the altar of their future.

For all the ways we're prone to overthinking ministry, conditioned to see it as a checklist of duties rather than a natural expression of love, clinging to the classical "missionary" framework where only some are called and the rest of us dodged the bullet, Cory and I are discovering that one of the most meaningful gifts we can offer the kingdom is our reputation.

It appears we've been called to the ministry of helping felons and drifters find suitable employment. Now and then, it actually works out. But it doesn't happen without a cost. When we look power-holders in the eye and ask them to take a chance on a friend, we know we can't make promises. We know it might all fall apart. More often than not, it does.

But maybe *this one* is different.

Maybe if we all squeeze in and surround this man who wants to believe he's capable, he'll rise up and prove it to be true.

Maybe as we look her in the eye and say, "I trust you," she'll prove herself trustworthy.

We're invited to cash in our gold-star, pop-processed reputation for the counterculture character of Jesus, who defends the cause of the oppressed. In a world that wears cynicism like a coat of arms, let's take up the Pollyanna belief that every person is entitled to be the object of surprise and delight. It sounds so simple, we run the risk of minimizing its significance.

Sure, it might end up a raging disaster.

But we are not allowed to judge people for being unemployed if we aren't willing to do everything in our capacity to help them secure a steady job. In his magnificent book *Tattoos on the Heart*, Father Gregory Boyle wrote, "Here is what we seek: a compassion that can stand in awe at what the poor have to carry rather than stand in judgment at how they carry it."[3]

The poor among us have so much more to offer society than their plasma. As we begin to see our kinship with them, all of us with flaws and so much potential, we'll take that risk. Slowly, we'll redefine success, seeing one another through the eyes of grace that never stops hoping.

Will our reputation be smudged up in the process? With any luck, yes.

6

GATHER

New Testament faith cannot be practiced in private. Either the faith will destroy the isolation, or the isolation will destroy the faith.

—*DIRTY FAITH*, DAVID Z. NOWELL[1]

IF THIS WERE 2011 and you were a therapist asking me to free-associate about "community," I would rattle off a string of words about my town and the importance of going to church. For me "community" was a noun in two forms. Primarily, it could be distilled down to Google Maps coordinates, a voting precinct, or the public library where paying overdue fees was (and remains) my personal civic duty.

It was also a hazy, best-case scenario from God, a hope for the faithful. As a Christian I was called to a community of like-minded saints, where we would spur one another on and sharpen each other's iron and stuff. When it came down to it, it meant I had to go to church, not because my salvation hinged on it, but because God said it was important. I did my best to believe him, generously expanding my definition of community beyond my best friends (mirror images of me) to include the slightly less-identical folks with whom I shared a pew and participated in actively hiding the worst of ourselves.

I massaged truth around my standard perspective, then passed it like the plate. *Community is good. Community is important. See how good we are at community?*

When God swept in and uprooted us, it wasn't just money and my big ideas that ended up at the curb. Everything was up for grabs, especially my ideas about authentic community.

What I know now is that sometimes surrender means letting go, and other times it means letting *in*.

Zip Codes

Not long before we left the farm, we were gathered into a small, hodgepodge group of people desperate for new life to be breathed into our dried-up faith. We came from different places, sharing no more than an inkling that when it came to God and his kingdom, up was actually down, and straight lines were mangled into what looked like chaos but was actually freedom.

These were some rebel thinkers, ready to face the ways they'd been wrong and preferring not to do it alone. I was instantly at home among them.

Every Monday night, we gathered wherever we were able, most often at a church none of us attended (perhaps one of the most redemptive aspects of our gathering), to share a meal and our lives.

Because we were a conglomeration of the creatively repressed, we routinely pulled together pitch-in meals that made us feel like royalty. Week after week we doled out high fives and went back for seconds while the men stroked their beards and occasionally even rubbed their bellies. (It was awkward for everyone.)

Dinner was reason enough to show up.

But the most beautiful outgrowth of our gathering was that it offered a taste of true community. Discussion was vibrant and often inconclusive, with spouses sometimes falling on opposite sides of a particular issue. Spoiler alert: Cory and I formed the most notorious duo for this sort of "spirited" debate.

Though our desire for more of God was at our epicenter, we'd grown lax in the rules of the faith we were raised with. We prayed before our meal, but the emphasis was on our unrefined gratitude for his goodness among us. We often asked one of the kids to pray, which occasionally resulted in riotous NASCAR chants or unintelligible gobbledygook. We read books that brought all our doubts bubbling to the surface. Does God still do miracles? My answer—just look around this circle, goober. We were inappropriate often, easily sidetracked always. We created our own offshoot of what Christian community could be. In the haven of ordinary Monday evenings, we found freedom and, if we were extra lucky, two top-notch desserts.

Soon enough it wasn't primarily about those two hours at all. We were in the thick of life together, committed to encouraging one another as God kept messing up our once-placid lives and stressing all of us out. To illustrate, in the span of just one year, two of the men left positions as full-time pastors, another guy filled one of those vacancies, and Cory became the unlikeliest jail chaplain in the history of ever.

These were the people who not only accepted the sharp

veering of our lives, but understood it. They were our row-diest fans. In the scheme of things they were the ones on the sidelines with face paint—and probably some bare-chested body paint because the men shared not a single ounce of shame among them.

They were the cheerleaders to all of our misunderstood unconvention. When necessary they ran out to the field, scooped us up, and hauled us off. They tended our wounds, gave us cool water, then swatted us on the rear and sent us back out where we belonged. We did the same for them.

None of us shared a property line, but we were all neighbors. And we loved each other.

It was all so piercingly beautiful that just writing about it right now has me sobbing conspicuously into two tiny beverage napkins (one for each eye) at our bustling local coffee shop while I type. I can't even tell you how brave and kind these people are.

What we experienced was a glimpse of the kingdom of God and our place in its expanse.

In one another we saw that there's a big difference between living in *a* community and living *in* community. The two aren't related. They don't even share a zip code.

The problem—and I'm taking liberties with that p-word—is that it filled Cory and me with a longing to carry a similarly arms-wide, bare-your-ugly, come-as-you-are-and-be-fed soul of restorative community into our new, uh, *community*.

Rather than getting too mired (there was definitely *some* miring) in our old ways of thinking about it for months, asking everyone and their cousin's babysitter for advice, "praying" about it (code for more procrastinating), making lists and ledgers, and creating a special Facebook page, we started with this: How can we show up and be the most authentic version of ourselves?

In the weeks leading up to the move, before we knew a soul on our street and when we were still operating haphazardly as a ball of jangled nerves, our Monday night group, none of whom lived in our new city, linked arms and walked with us into the wide unknown.

Surprising no one, we made our grand entrance the only way we knew how—with large quantities of delicious food. We hauled a grill to the park across the street from our new home, fired it up, and wondered if anyone else would trickle over.

Sure enough, teenagers and kids came out of the woodwork, joining us there on the splintered picnic benches. Over the unifying force of hot dogs, across tables etched with ill-fated promises, we saw past heavy eyeliner and bad haircuts and caught a peek into their hearts. Because community isn't paved with one-way streets, they did the same. They saw exactly as much of us as we were willing to offer.

Photos from that evening somehow ended up as the screen-saver for our TV. (Technology-related details remain fuzzy to me.) They scroll across the screen and I think, *Man, God wasn't playing around.* He could have sent a different crowd to the pavilion. He could have sent people just like us, people who'd have made us feel as safely bubble-wrapped and at ease as we were back on the farm, maybe some white middle-classers or a couple of the young, spit-shined families in the neighborhood.

He could have sent no one at all, and we would have been just fine.

As it was, he sent a small posse of misfits, kids flunking their classes and flinging cuss words and walnuts (don't ask). Knowing us for less than fifteen minutes, they immediately started gossiping and oversharing. When their mamas screamed like banshees for them to come the bleep home, they flat ignored them.

As an entry point into our brand-new neighborhood, God sent people *just like us*. Rebel hearts longing for home.

Walking Toward the Pain

Though I'd prefer to interpret "neighbor" as my family or, at most, the people on the other side of our property line, Jesus had a way of kicking borders and boundaries to sea. He mashed definitions and stirred people together. He said we were all the same, and that we belonged to one another.

He lunched with jailbirds.

He chatted at the water cooler with hookers.

Knowing the oxymoronic futility of loving people from a safe distance, Jesus lived and moved and snacked on olives and wine, wearing a 24/7 love as fierce as it was undeserved. This love offered little respect for the tidiness of home-drawn boundaries. It was tangled. Complicated. Messy.

That's how Jesus spent his life on earth—schooling the shady characters, the unusual suspects, the poor, the grieving, the needy, the broken, the "bad influences," the ones who make people like me jittery and unsure. He showed up in their messes, then stuck around, operating from a place of undeniable, relentless pursuit.

Where does this leave the girl whose every minute is spent with people nearly identical to herself? What if almost everyone in her circle already knows God? What's the point of living parallel lives, absent the messy crosshatches and scribbles that happen when cultures and social strata and worldviews blend? I'm asking for a friend.

Though many of our neighbors in our new community lived lives very similar to ours, just as many did not. I was stunned to realize my tools were all wrong for the job—money, security, and mad middle-class life skills for achievement and stability.

We'd been so wrong for so long.

We still struggle against ourselves. Our faulty view of the world and our position in it remain a nagging problem. We rack up missteps the way some people collect baseball cards or Coke points. We made big mistakes on the front end of our journey, which is bad enough, but, like a child who doesn't learn her lesson, we continue to make some of them.

There was the time we bluntly accused a temporary guest—a recent visitor at the county jail—of stealing our house key, only to find it a few days later right where we'd left it.

We've said no when we should've said yes, and yes when we should've run for the hills. We've hopped up on our high horse and willed friends to aspire to our stable, middle-class ways, only to crash and burn into the unexpected reality that they were in our lives to teach *us*, not the other way around.

Then there was the fateful day in early fall when I invited strangers into my bathroom. I'd overheard grousing outside the living room window about one of the small kids in their caravan urgently needing to do some business. Inserting myself like only a woman desperate to know her neighbors would, I flung the front door open and invited them in. My intentions were nothing but good. I wanted to help, and I happened to have a vacant bathroom.

My helpfulness ended when I bungled through a stretch of

awkward silence with the mom by blurting out, "So, are you expecting?"

She mumbled back, "Uh, no," and gestured to the tiny, eight-month-old baby *in her arms.*

You get my point here. Please don't take your cues on fostering community from me. Woe be unto the world led by Shannan Martin.

But therein lies the whole flipping mystery. God says we get to be a part of his grand scheme to redeem his people. He doesn't need the help of us broken bandits. He wants it. He loves us enough to invite us into the thrill of his redemption, where we're all made more worthy. He chooses us against all the evidence proving we're not to be trusted. He welcomes our mess then asks us to do the same for each other.

This morning I laced my sneakers, left my phone on the nightstand, and headed out into the neighborhood.

I walked south, past a banged-up, better-days rental house. We have watched its landlord corner vulnerable people in a market where most see them only as risk. This guy swoops in and offers them a roof and roach-filled walls, charges them more than they could ever afford, and chalks it up as an off-brand of charity. *At least they have a place to live.*

But that's not the most shocking part.

The shocking part is that this man, with his dusty work pants and a disarming kindness in his eyes, is cracked from the same mold as I, bearing the image of God while he goes to church and fumbles on the job, believing in his heart that what he's doing is right. I've found him unsuitable for my love, from the "safe" distance that exists when you know *of* someone but don't really *know* him.

I still don't know him. But my heart was softened when God, in his infinite love for both of us, placed me on the same street just as he crossed, his arms full, a 3 Musketeers bar balanced between his teeth. He knocked on a sad-looking screen door splayed from its hinges, then entered. In the smallness of the moment, I knew. He's human. Flesh and bone, just going about his day. He knows grief and joy just like the rest of us. He tries. He fails. He might care in ways I haven't considered.

If Jesus lived on my street, I imagine he would follow closely behind him, knock on the very same door, and ask for half of his candy bar. Based on all I've seen of Jesus, I believe in the guts of my guts that he might invite this man to drop his handwritten lease agreements and his eviction notices and follow him. This person I feel justified in judging is the woman at the well; the tax collector in the sycamore tree; the Jewish terrorist, Saul, hell-bent on persecuting the church. I know, against every ounce of my modern-day wisdom and good-girl tendencies, this landlord is exactly who Jesus would choose for his team.

He didn't inherit or get stuck with his disciples. It wasn't pity. He tracked them down. He didn't witness to them. These were his buds. They lived life together. They belonged to each other.

He chooses the all-wrong to bring his kingdom down to earth.

He grabs hold of flawed people and transforms them with his full-throttle love.

Just like he found a privileged, prideful woman living at the sunny end of a long country lane and wrecked her quiet life for his glory, showing her the ways she'd been an oppressor and loving her anyway.

What Jesus didn't do was surround himself with plastic, churchy folk. He wanted every bit of everyone, especially the ugly parts. He wanted the guts and blood and dirt and snot and all the things we're so used to cleaning up or covering up before we step one toe out of hiding.

He wanted the raw opposite of God, not a gaggle of puffed-up pretenders.

He wants the same today.

God gives us the job of loving him with all our hearts and loving our neighbors well. Not modern-American "well enough," but messy, swerve-toward-the-ditch, shuck your coat, purge your world, give in your lack, Jesus-brand of "well." Another way to say it is, love them exactly as much as we love ourselves. It feels downright impossible, because, holy cow, do I ever love myself. I love myself so much, I often doubt there are reserves left to give.

Thankfully, Jesus taught us how to do this love thing. It doesn't mean it's easy or straightforward, just that we have a goes-everywhere teacher, a personal grace tutor. It means this dance is more complex than we want to think, but also much simpler. We're tasked with learning the hardest moves, but if we let him lead, he won't let us face-plant on the ballroom floor.

Not long ago my family shared a meal with one of our neighbors. We'd known Jason for a while, though our connections were mostly superficial. Still, there was something about his baby face and his easy smile that tugged at my heart. He was one of the people I always searched for as I walked the neighborhood.

Jason had been in and back out of the jail for a quick stint, then had gone quiet. It had been months since we'd seen him last, and I wondered about him often. Having grown used to the transience of our community, I assumed he was long gone.

When Cory's phone buzzed with his text, I jumped at the chance to reconnect with him. "Invite him to dinner. It's only tomato soup, but maybe he'll come."

By the time he showed up, the soup had gone cold. I quickly reheated a bowl and ladled a little more into Cory's bowl so Jason wouldn't feel awkward eating alone. After a bit of small talk, in my usual fashion, I retreated to our bedroom, just off the kitchen, to fold some laundry while he and Cory talked. Why had he suddenly popped back into our lives? Our interactions with him had always been friendly, but casual. And he'd never been a visitor in our home.

Pairing socks, I trained my ear to the dining room table. Between the sounds of spoons scraping bowls, Jason asked, "So, how do you know God is real?" This was a young man who had never shown a moment of interest in talking about God or being vulnerable with us in any way. He had sought Cory out that evening, which we knew meant something, but I honestly assumed it would be more along the lines of a more typical, "Hey, so-and-so got locked up. Can you visit him for me?" We did not see this coming.

I dropped the whites and joined them at the table, not wanting to miss a word of whatever might happen next.

The three of us sat there for an hour or so, wading through our brother's struggle for belief. "I know there's something more than this. I feel it in my heart that God is real, but how do you know for sure?" So we shared about how hearing from God isn't just the privilege of people like us, chaplains and middle-class moms. It's for everyone, including him.

"You reached out to us tonight, Jason, out of the blue. That was God speaking to you. You heard him. And you came!" His expression paused in concentrated intent, then broke into a wide smile. *He was getting it.*

It's fundamentally game-changing to be present in the lives of friends who stumble along without a well-worn rule book on how life should look. They're so unencumbered, with their sloppy, disorganized faith. They might not be able to name the books of the Bible, but they sure do believe it was written for them. There are no code words, no secret checklists, no balancing, weighing, stacking mine against theirs.

All they know for sure is their need. They know sorrow and lack. They dare to believe, just like the woman at the well, that *maybe* God is who he says he is.

I want their stripped-down, daily-bread faith. I am pulled to their turbulent sea.

Want to know what will cut to the heart of soul-filling community faster than anything else? Look a meth addict in the eyes and tell her you've been a cheater. Invite a homeless drunk into your kitchen and serve him boxed mac and cheese with love, remembering with fresh clarity the way you've chosen to pitch your tent on the riverbank of shame. Watch tears of regret and dread drip off the tattooed face of a felon and offer back some of the ways you've bankrupted your own freedom.

God invites us to stare long and hard at our shared ruin, knowing we'll walk away kindred. It's through our cracks that we fall into each other. It's through relationships that we know him more.

Spitting Mad

Some people struggle to believe God really loves them. They have trouble seeing him as patient with their mistakes or charmed by their incessant humanity.

For whatever reason I have more of the opposite problem. I view God as highly entertained by us. Does he love all our decisions? Nope. But the only option is for him to be relentlessly *with* us, well aware of our propensity to veer off course, but too busy being crazy about us to waste time wishing we would stop being so . . . human.

Also I might suffer a touch from over-esteeming my general charm. When I graduated from high school, oh, a hundred or so years ago, I felt bone-deep pity for the poor teachers who would have to go on living without the pleasurable presence of the winsome class of '94.

Though I've warmed to reality a little since then, and despite being more aware of my sinfulness than I care to be, I see all of us humans as funny and interesting, prone to make a mess of things, yet, thanks to the grace of God, not the least bit smite-worthy.

Isaiah tells of a slightly less rosy reality.

Guns blazing, he launches into his lengthy, sixty-six-chapter tome with prophetic words about God's disgust with Judah's put-on attempts at being good enough. The second half of the first chapter reads particularly like a spit-flinging tirade:

> "I am sick of your burnt offerings. . . . I want no more of your pious meetings. I hate your new moon celebrations. . . . They are a burden to me. I cannot stand them! When you lift up

your hands in prayer, I will not look. . . . I will not listen. . . .
Get your sins out of my sight." (Isa. 1:11–16)

And then just before what feels like an inevitable mic-drop
from Isaiah, we read this:

Learn to do good. Seek justice. Help the oppressed. Defend
the cause of orphans. Fight for the rights of widows. "Come
now, let's settle this," says the Lord. "Though your sins are
like scarlet, I will make them as white as snow." (Isa. 1:17–18)

We get the drift.

If we're not taking up the cause of the least and bearing it as
our own, God covers his ears. He hides his eyes from us. Our
check-marked church attendance is a burden to him. Our lives
ring hollow, a dead cymbal clang, if we can't get on board with
love and extend it to the marginalized. Apart from his rules,
we're playing church. And he's not interested.

It seems impossible that this stuff matters so much to him.

This wasn't what I was taught in my thirty-odd years
of Christian training. It wasn't at the center of my religious
instruction. If anything, it was a footnote, a theory, a "parable"
(read: cute, Christian fairy tale). This idea of actively caring
for and defending the oppressed was entirely foreign to me. I
didn't even know the oppressed. The oppressed were in Cuba
or maybe Detroit.

Isaiah wasn't relevant to me. It was for those blasted Israelites.

I thought caring for the least meant caring about them.
Who's heartless enough to not care about poor people? This
caring *about* required little more than an occasional thought. It

was never a "bring them into your home, feed them hot food, drive them all over Timbuktu, and don't ask questions" sort of caring. It was a check in the mail or a lump in my throat on mission-emphasis Sunday. It involved zero relationship and paltry sacrifice. It certainly didn't leave room for my life to be changed for the better by them and the ways they would care for me.

Community, in its purest form, is anything but pure. It's noisy. Inconvenient. It demands we come to painful terms with the persistent cultural lies of independence and self-sufficiency, both of which run contrary to the gospel. It demands what my friend Becca Stanley, an urban missionary in Atlanta, calls "dignified interdependence."[2]

To be in community is to be painfully aware of our own unlovability but to offer ourselves anyway. Community simply can't share space with masks or props. They're mutually exclusive. They cancel each other out.

How do we do this? How can we possibly live in true community with our neighbors in the face of socioeconomic disparities, language barriers, cultural differences, heightened racial tensions, and the boring reality that many of them move in and back out again before we can even learn their names?

The answer is stunning in its simplicity.

We dare to believe we are the most broken people we know, and we refuse to turn away when faced with blinding proof. We remind ourselves that no one actually needs us, especially God.

More than anything, we stop fixating on how to love our neighbor as an entity separate from us and simply start living like a neighbor. In my family's life this has included innumerable everyday things, not limited to the following:

- Accepting the request to watch a neighbor's daughter when she wound up in a scheduling pinch. More importantly, it meant asking her to return the favor. Nothing makes community of neighbors faster than broadcasting your neediness.

- Sending our kids to the Title I public school at the end of the street and making the tiny, aging congregation at the end of the block our home church. I'll talk more about both in later chapters, but suffice it to say, there's something to be said for blooming where we're planted and having skin in the game among institutions that serve widely and without discrimination. Community is, at its essence, unique lives lived in tandem.

- Sitting around a late-summer campfire with neighbors who speak limited English. As someone who abhors awkward silence even more than small talk, I felt visceral pain that evening. But we cobbled together small bits of important information; we smiled over a tiny camping grill; we watched our kids run together crazed and giddy in the moonlight. *What differences?* My neighbor had the courage to attempt my language, so I offered the same with immeasurably less grace and skill. We took risks together. Vulnerability is the glue of community.

- Attending meetings—neighborhood association meetings, race-relation meetings, planning meetings, PTO meetings, outreach meetings. With no agenda other than the one on the table in front of us, we found that the playing field was leveled, and we walked away with friends whose names we knew. When we put on our shoes and actually go places, friendships are born *and* things are accomplished. Viva la meeting!

- Buying Popsicles in bulk and consciously resisting the urge to sink cute picket fencing along our perimeter. The path to community, at least for our kids, is an unimpeded stretch of yard between our stocked freezer and our neighbors' brand-new trampoline.

- Fumbling my way through an exercise class at a local studio, buying groceries at the closer but slightly more expensive grocery store, starting a book club with local acquaintances who have become fast friends, saying yes to the bow-tied man who asked me, in my busiest season, to write a column for the local newspaper. Community begins when we make space in our lives for others and walk heavy on the paths between us.

When we stopped gravitating only to people who reminded us of ourselves, our community grew in width and depth. Rather than concede to our basest anxieties that we would never again know friendship born of the everyday mundane, God has cooked us up a special batch of magic. Stirred together with actual neighbors, folks across town, women twice my age and a decade younger, new moms and wizened grammies, trailblazers for our city and advocates for the needy, blended families and cross-cultural soul mates, mixed with dear souls from across the political aisle, unchurched friends, smokers and clowns and intellectuals who make my gray matter feel rigid and rusty, *this* is the community I was created for, where our ordinary knocking-around binds us into the double helix of eternity's DNA.

I came so close to missing out on this gift I never knew I wanted.

If I've learned anything at all in the past three years, it's that the shortest routes to relationships are carved when everyone takes two giant steps past the gates of their comfort and toward each other.

It has been worth it every time.

7

OPEN THE DOOR

Hospitality is the virtue of a great soul that cares for the whole universe through the ties of humanity.
—*HOSPITALITY*, LOUIS, CHEVALIER DE JAUCOURT[1]

LORI AND MIKE first came to my table on one of those frigid November evenings where the light had seeped out of the day well before dinner and entertaining was the last thing I felt like doing.

I stood at the stove in day-two yoga pants and stirred the pot with my longest-handled spoon.

What was I thinking?

Just as I began hoping they might bail, they swept through the door. In a rush of biting cold, a swirl of cigarette smoke, and the tinny laughter of the anxious, they defied the good sense of this risk-leery world and showed up.

Before that night we'd shared no more than two minutes of conversation. We were complete strangers without a single degree of Kevin Bacon between us, and I was equal parts thrilled and terrified. The threat of awkwardness loomed large in the dark hours ahead of us. Sharing no common vocabulary and having life experiences that overlapped only in slivers, what on earth would we talk about? How would we possibly connect?

Lori handed me an eight-dollar coconut pie and a frosted blue votive holder. "I hope you like it. I didn't know what your colors were," and I was leveled, my pride and my stupid ideas about who belongs where falling in a heap on the kitchen floor.

As I passed plates and served salad, my dormant hostess jitters flared and sputtered. Was the pasta too sticky? What was their opinion on tomatoes (so polarizing!), and do they really prefer the garlic bread slightly burnt, or are they just being nice?

Across the table sat my eight-year-old daughter. Adjacent to her sat a man she had never seen before, with Gothic lettering inscribed across his Adam's apple and the f-word emblazoned down the length of his forearm. For the first time in my life, I questioned the hours we'd spent honing our kids' early reading skills. We spoke about small things, Lori's blue eyes tracking Mike's. Their hearts were undeniably kind, their souls battered and torn. My soul recognized theirs as world-weary kin.

From the perspective of my warm city kitchen and the goodness unfolding inside its walls, any risk it had required to get to that distinct moment was worth it. I always knew I wanted to entertain friends. It was fun. It was easy. But the abundant life asks more of us. I had no idea the leap from stranger to friend was only as long as the eight minutes it took to boil pasta, or that my life would be made richer once I yielded to the unifying power of the unfancy dinner table.

Stranger Danger

If community is the heartbeat of the gospel, hospitality is the hand that opens the door and waves it in. Like a thick slather of cream cheese frosting across a yeasty cinnamon roll, hospitality adds the sweetest layer. There's no point in having one without the other.

The home I grew up in was the end of the line for many end-of-the-liners, a last-resort respite for unlikely sojourners and fugitives alike. Throughout my at-home years there were single moms with babies who'd been kicked out of their homes, a lonely near-stranger with sallow eyes on a rented hospital bed in the living room, lanky high school boys at odds with their parents, our own grandma with her wheelchair and fluffy curls who rotated among her children. None was more memorable than Carla, an eccentric woman on the lam from an abusive husband. We stowed her away, hiding her stuff in our shed, hypervigilant whenever we heard tires crunching up the lane.

God knew living together in harmony would sometimes feel like knitting a blanket with one broken needle and two skeins of steel wool, or like training a cat to keep banker's hours. He likes us needy and maybe even a little frustrated. When we abide in the ordinary holiness of misunderstandings and disappointments, our own rough edges are somehow buffed down. In the close proximity to one another, he's always among us. And nothing pulls us closer than passing dishes around the table or sitting hip to hip on the couch.

Jesus spoke about hospitality often, but trumping his words were his actual life and the way he spent it. He was the king of traipsing from town to town, eating with scandalous people and long-lost souls, mending their wounds from his seat at their table. Through the clatter of plates and the din of easy, grub-time conversation, hearts are fused and burdens lifted. He embodied hospitality in the precise way he *is* hope, mercy, wisdom, and justice. The fact that he was always inviting himself over and showing up at parties points us to the significance of living hospitably and the vulnerability it requires.

As usual, Jesus disguises our most challenging work as nearly mundane. *Invite people—especially strangers—into your home. No big deal.*

I can handle the "people" part.

It's the "stranger" bit that makes my pits sweaty. I happen to love inviting friends over for dinner. I've hosted everything from brunches to baby showers to season premiere dinner parties. ("Clear eyes, full hearts, can't lose!") There have been innumerable elaborate dinners with close girlfriends where I hauled out the thrift store china and unabashedly displayed my culinary chops with multiple courses involving whole vanilla beans and obscure grains.

But strangers? No one does that. *It's weird, God. I'm just being honest.*

New beginnings always start with seeking. And seeking is often the answer to restlessness. Not long before we sold the farm, God began liberating us from our small view of hospitality. This freedom showed up quietly at first, in the cracks of our ordinary life. Our unrest was hazy at the edges and tender in the middle. It lacked both shape and clarity. We were faced with a question we couldn't answer for ourselves, a nagging hunch that it was time to reach in and grab all the junk we'd accumulated in our privileged corner and toss it out. Maybe the politicians, the civic groups, the churchy folks, and our elders had taught us things that were not true, seeds that eventually bloomed into superiority and disregard, both of which dull our ability to love.

Without our knowing how it had happened, something shifted. We realized we were no longer the good news, and it was likely we had never been. Where we once saw ourselves as the responsible owners of a house we'd earned, we began to see our actual position—as tenants.

Perhaps because we were already mired in a constitutional confusion, bone-deep and endlessly murky, we didn't have the wherewithal to obsessively overthink our next moves. Too emotionally spent to worm our way around it, we went looking for opportunity to practice this new view of hospitality.

In the agonizing months while we waited for our farm to sell, here's a sampling of what we found:

- Our Sunday school class invited ourselves to the rec room of a nearby, low-income apartment complex, brought a bunch of food, and told the tenants we hoped they would join us. Along with twenty others, Ricki showed up. She very nearly fainted from delight over my friend Dora's strawberry Jell-O salad, and after her second trip to the dessert table, she looked me straight in the eye and said, without an edge of sarcasm, "I don't deserve food this good."
- Cory's then-boss introduced us to his ragtag group of friends who lived homeless on a makeshift river camp.

I was stunned to discover there were homeless people within our county lines. Stunned! We got to know them and all their quirks. We saw them, then found it impossible to unsee.

- Students from the alternative school where Cory worked began trickling home with him for dinner. On one memorable occasion, after I'd pulled out all the stops mashing potatoes and hand-rolling meatballs, one of them shared the highlight of his day as the turkey sandwich and Fritos he'd had for lunch.

Our path toward Jesus' heart was the length of a dinner table. It was there that we began to come face-to-face with a rescuer we had never known, one who hunts his kids down in the dead of night, ready to stop the world and street-fight for them. This Jesus adored the ones we despised. When he said, "The last shall be first," he was not being cute. He'd take us split and bleeding, reeking and raw. He preferred it that way. Until we began to make friends of strangers and see the ways we so cleanly aligned with their frailty, I hadn't considered that it might actually be true.

And yet.

Four years later, it's honestly still hard for me. It's still not second nature, or even fourth. I know I'm not alone.

We tell ourselves it's because our homes are not enough—big enough, clean enough, cute enough.

We might even begin to believe our home is *too* much. I can't absorb the jab of regret quickly enough when someone mired in poverty says my home is pretty. Quick to tamp it all down, I tell the truth—almost everything in it is on its second or third life. I want to wave the compliment away, change the subject. It makes me so uncomfortable.

Regardless of the visitor, whether I'm feeling the itch of scarcity or abundance, I can't shake the feeling that hospitality is somehow, secretly, about me.

Chief among my troubling, me-centric excuses is this—I'm an introvert. I like life quiet. Hospitality isn't my spiritual gift. Many show hospitality with more skill and ease than I do, and they should use that gift for all its worth. But loving our neighbor isn't optional. It's imperative. Jesus tells us *this is how we love him* (Matt. 25:40).

Peter encourages us to "cheerfully" share our home with others (1 Peter 4:9), and it's all I can do some days to serve my own unpredictable brood with a half-smile. All this means is that I need to keep practicing, and spread out against this long life, I've got time.

Last year a woman we'd recently met arrived at our door fresh from jail, a few minutes after midnight, her life in a black Hefty bag. A recovering addict, she'd spent most of the previous three years separated from her young children, cycling in and out of incarceration as she cycled in and out of mainlining meth. Finally free, anxiety radiated off her in shock waves.

I showed her to our guest quarters, which happened to be Silas's mattress in clean, mismatched sheets, hauled down to the floor of the cluttered toy room. There was a time I would have been horrified to offer so little. It would have mortified me to make this my offering.

I might have said no.

But it seems the best way to welcome a broken neighbor is by hanging up the charade that we are somehow more whole.

We don't need bigger homes and better furniture to do this well. If anything, we need less stuff that's more frayed at the edges. Central to the way I steward my home and love my neighbor is my willingness to expose my messes, scars, and the stubborn humanity I can't seem to keep at bay.

And if I'm willing to go there, what's a stack of dirty dishes or Aunt Lon's ugly, hand-me-down sofa?

When we grip our ideals about hospitality too tightly, we risk withholding what is actually needed. What our friend needed that night was encouragement, a hot bath, and a glass of iced tea. What she needed for the nights that followed were space to process a future that finally belonged to her, and a cherished place of acceptance among a very imperfect family.

That's the essence of hospitality. Who cares if you burned the soup or if the guest is incomprehensibly averse to garlic? So what if the floors are swept or if I opted to stay in my yoga pants? We're all a mess, but while a bunch of messes should amount to more than we can stomach, it somehow has the opposite effect. *Where two or more jacked-up lives are gathered in the holy name of loving like Jesus and telling the truth, there am I in their midst.*

Real hospitality is more like the widow's mite than Solomon's purple robes. It's the sharing of manna—that ordinary miracle— and the faith to believe we can love big with just a little.

Fire and Spice

When Cory discovered his calling as the chaplain for our county jail, we weren't prepared for the ways the inmates would teach us the basics of hospitality: ignoring our differences and hopping the scales to that precarious place of unbalance where we're all in this together somewhere at the bottom, sifting through the hand life dealt us. Resting in that tender place of me-too-ness, the community of sinners makes way for the communion of saints.

It started with his shoes.

If you could see them, you wouldn't be impressed. They're run-of-the-mill, nondescript hybrid athletic/dress shoes that, by design, consistently miss the mark. *You're brown. Are you a dress shoe? But you have racing stripes and overeager treading . . .* Whatever. After a decade in suits and ties, if the man wants to wear brown gym shoes to work, let him. You know?

The inmates could not get enough. They were instantly smitten. (My loose interpretation of their enthusiasm.) For the first time in his life, Cory found himself on the cutting edge of shoe fashion. It was a boon! It was ridiculous.

While we law-abiding citizens perpetuate the practice of "welcoming" folks into our homes with the requirement that they remove their shoes so as not to soil our floors (our floors!), these guys, most of them indelibly shaped by poverty, knew the floors were never the point. The shoes were the point, or, more specifically, the guy wearing them.

These men were criminals. They'd committed egregious offenses like slandering their neighbor, coveting what wasn't theirs, gossiping about the dude down the street, and then some.

When the bearded, brown-shoed guy showed up un-announced in their cinder block home, they could have been basting in the shame of whatever had landed them there in their dust-colored scrubs, or making a mental checklist of why the chaplain was somehow better than them. I'm guessing they weren't pondering how narrowly they had missed each other's fates, or all the ways their sins were the same as his, though all of it would have been true. Rather than catalog their differences, they simply made room for him at their table, no questions asked.

He went to make his home among men who were despised, overlooked, and underserved. How was it possible? How can any of us ever hope to accomplish this grafting of vastly different lives without delineating "them" from "us," saying, essentially, "I am well; you are not"?

The hard truth is, in order to love them, he first had to know them.

Tastes in sports or music or beer, political leanings, gang affiliations, and religious backgrounds faded into the background of a gray room where the furniture was bolted down and the men were hungry.

The literal breaking of bread is the surest path to fellowship.

Only at mealtime are the nonessentials shoved from the table so hunger can meet its end. Only then do the senses take over, allowing our brains and our obtrusive opinions a quick siesta. *We'll come back to that later. What's for lunch?*

Sadly, the lunch menu in jail is always the same—jail food. But misery never outgrows its pull for companionship, so the men sit together on metal stools and grouse about the soggy bologna sandwiches, the mushy beans, the "choke bread" (cornbread so dry you choke). They scrape plastic spoons against plastic trays, and they eat, distracting one another and themselves with talk of baby mamas, the kids they miss, the visitors they wish would show up. They might even run and grab the Bible from under their bunk to show the chaplain what they've underlined, their eyes shimmering with the fullness of God's love while they describe his goodness in words ripe with sincerity and the occasional f-bomb.

But seriously, the food. Think school cafeteria food—long before its recent revolution—only 90 percent less flavorful. It's highly processed and mashed into different shapes, day after day after day, on disposable table service that must be fully accounted for when mealtime is over.

If you're lucky, you have someone putting cash on your books so you can buy an overpriced box of salt and pepper packets, or even better, a bottle of hot sauce.

These become your prized possessions, tangible tokens of pride, the equivalent of wearing the newest sneakers on the schoolyard or driving a car with chrome rims. You hoard this artificial-everything magic that turns "cat head" (don't ask) into something negligibly edible. Condiments and seasonings are bottled proof that you have someone on the outside looking after you. You belong to someone.

It is your currency, and you track it like a hawk.

Hot sauce is the very best you have to offer, one of the few things you truly own, your pearl of great price. So what do you do? You invite the stranger to your table. You pass that bottle to the bearded chaplain in the sick shoes and watch as the water turns to wine.

When Jesus told his disciples to set a place at their tables for folks at the margins, it wasn't meant as an exercise in proving their sincerity to follow after him. It wasn't an opportunity to earn extra credit. He told us to do this because he crazy-loves us. He wants to return us to the people created in his image and move us away from a world that values the wrong things. He wants to offer us the beauty of learning from his chosen companions and to find ourselves in the fibers of their stories.

If we can't get on board with this off-kilter framework for

building our community, we risk missing one of the fundamentals of the very gospel we say we live by. When we seclude ourselves, wrapped so tightly in what brings us comfort that we can't see the uninvited or ignored, or when we do see them but decide they're too much trouble, we relinquish our right to experience the richness of his goodness.

But if we shuck off our easy tendencies and sacrifice for a wanderer, we taste the kingdom of God, sweet, salty, and spicy enough to make our eyes water.

DWTN (Dancing with the Neighbors)

My skewed view of hospitality as linear and one-directional is slowly blossoming into a pulsing, breathing, tangled thing that moves in every direction at once.

Hospitality is the tango. It always takes two.

The part of me powered by middle-class independence would rather do the Macarena. Or maybe the hula. When it comes to hospitality, I'm so much happier on the side of "giver." Not only does it allow me to project the illusion of managing my own game with flawless ease; it gives me all the warm, fuzzy, helper feelings. It's nice to meet someone's needs. It feels good, because it *is* good.

Unfortunately we can't extend genuine hospitality until we're comfortable on the receiving end as well. It has to be a two-way street. Lacking this duality—this freedom—it becomes all about us ("*See what I did for you?*") or all about them ("*Don't you appreciate my kindness?*").

A few weeks ago I traveled to Nebraska to speak at a women's brunch. Though it was my first time there, I found myself at home among both the wide-stretched landscape and the salt-of-the-earth people. Still, getting from here to there was no easy feat. The trip clocked in at more than twelve hours, each way. After a ninety-minute drive to the airport, there were two flights, a long layover, and another drive ahead of me.

Because my introvert heart is a work-in-progress when it comes to receiving hospitality, I've made the conscious decision to actively seek opportunities to stay in the homes of my hosts when the opportunity presents itself. This doesn't come naturally to me, and somewhere into my tenth hour of travel to Nebraska, I began doubting my decision to stay in the home of a stranger.

I'm not sure when I'll stop sweating this stuff, but I shouldn't have worried.

My new friend greeted me with a smile late that night at the airport, her daughter in tow. We spent the drive to their home in easy conversation. That night, as my head hit the pillow, a fan whirring just for me in the corner, I sank into clean sheets with the streetlights of an unfamiliar town streaming through the blinds, unable to remember why I'd ever thought a sterile, anonymous hotel might be better. I accepted what was offered in the spirit of Christ's love and slept like a newborn.

Due to his chronic homelessness, Jesus was a Grand Champion at receiving hospitality. We see him in the homes of others, often the despised and harshly judged, and occasionally committing one of the gravest faux pas of our day—"Surprise! I'm coming over. And I'm hungry."

When he spotted wee Zacchaeus perched in that tree, craning his neck to catch a glimpse of this maybe-Messiah, Jesus knew he was needy. Among other things, Zacchaeus was in the market for a new reputation, a new job description, a massive change of heart, and a hearty glug of integrity.

Jesus could have made all of that happen in a flash, without ever sitting at his table as a friend. He could have touched that tree and shot healing straight up the bark. Or stood with Zacchaeus there in the dust and gently pointed out the ways he'd been living wrong. He could have sent someone else to befriend Zacchaeus or called in some favors and orchestrated a more savory career for him. Heck, Jesus could have made Zacchaeus taller, which, I imagine, would have been a change he would have harnessed for good.

What he did instead was call him down and invite himself to the table, where eyes meet and hearts soften. He kept himself small and fully human, then invited Zacchaeus to repentance through companionship and genuine love.

Jesus, God wearing flesh, walked his human feet into the home of a notorious, cheating sinner and offered the gifts of giving and receiving, the mutual communion where strangers become brothers.

When we focus too much on how we can help or serve our neighbors, we miss the fun of dancing with them. Only in the disco of everyday life do we witness the unfurling hope each of us brings to the floor. Only there, in the encompassing love of God among us, our blue-jeaned Jesus who walks our way and doesn't ever stop, can we be transformed by the acceptance and kindness found in unlikely places.

About That Sugar

A few months ago, Cory and his jailed comrades decided to throw a party celebrating an unprecedented achievement. A handful of them, most of whom hadn't finished high school or obtained a GED, had completed a legit college course along with some students from a local liberal arts college. It was a massive deal.

The class was called Inside/Out. It combined groups of people whose paths, for all the reasons we've discussed, probably shouldn't have crossed. In half of the seats: privilege, opportunity, education, stability, enriching life experiences. In the other half: generational poverty, splintered family trees, long histories of incarceration, and a sweeping reluctance to even consider the future.

The playing field was effectively leveled. They poured their souls into grueling discussions on racism, classism, justice, government, and God. Can you imagine the depth of this conversation, where every ear was tuned to listen? Each student walked in with one worldview and out with another. No heart was left unscathed.

For the final class, Cory pulled some strings and brought in doughnuts, because food is central to celebration. It's a universal truth. And if you're going to break bread together, that bread might as well be yeasty and sugar-glazed.

He had no idea the inmates had decided to make a contribution of their own, in the form of what's known as a "Sweet Slam."

The recipe, no doubt passed down for decades, remains a bit elusive. All we know for sure is that for weeks the guys with access to commisary stockpiled packaged snacks along the lines of Snickers and Milky Way candy bars, peanut butter cookies, brownies, hot cocoa mix, and other assorted sugar-laden junk foods. The day before the big event, they collaboratively pulverized their collection of goods, along with a bunch of jail-issued "sweet cakes," mashing them into a bar-like delicacy of artificially sweetened nonsense. Using a MacGyvered cardboard knife, they hacked it into rough-hewn hunks and doled it out to their classmates as a token of their highest level of esteem and honor.

It didn't matter that it officially depleted their stash. Rather, it fundamentally *did* matter. They had given in their lack, these men with checkered pasts and tattooed necks, these proud, hardened criminals pouring perfume on the feet of their Savior as they handed out the best they had to offer.

It would be a stretch to classify a Sweet Slam as bread, but I can't think of a more suitable replacement in a pinch. *Do this in remembrance of me.*

Hospitality at its best requires some risk. *Here's my heart, laid out on a chipped-up platter.* It's looking fear in the face—they might not show up, they might be disappointed in what I offer, they might not get me, they might insist on pretending—and walking in its direction anyway, even when it's not our strong suit, even when it amplifies our awkwardness and makes us feel a little jumpy. When we walk through the door of someone outside our social class and status, we accept our position as a wanderer in need of care. This is the essence of hospitality, and it goes both ways.

Hospitality is the gospel hidden deeply in our souls and in the corners of our homes. It's not Pinterest-worthy and requires a level of mutual trust. *Take me as I am, and I'll return the favor.* It's the unwavering belief that when I add your mess to my own, the place has never looked better.

Spill and Soak

That first November night with Lori and Mike turned into weeks, then months of late-night conversations, one cookie-baking marathon, and hundreds of agonizing pleas to God—*please keep their feet to your fire.* They talked about what it's like to live on the run from drug addiction, how it taunts you, tails you, tracks you down. Our conversations spanned life and God, regrets and dreams.

When Mike explained why his criminal gang, made famous for the fervor of their hatred, was full of "good people," I found the space to believe it might be true.

Over time we built the strangest sort of pseudo-family, readily recognizing ourselves in one another. We were partners in this mixed-up life and were lucky to count one another as friends.

These friends guided us in the dance of accepting hospitality and offering it back in turn. Through their vulnerability they reminded us of the peace found when we choose the undignified path of walking in frailty and living at the cliff edge of need.

We took turns spilling our guts there at the pockmarked dining table, sharing all the ways we'd failed to show up to the life God wrote for us and settled for less instead. They set the bar at bare-naked honesty. What could we do but match it? Aren't we all looking for the same exact things, to be accepted and loved in our brokenness?

I woke one morning before dawn to a scratching noise outside our bedroom window. There stood Mike, hunched over his shovel, in shoes that weren't waterproof, clearing our drive from snow we hadn't even known had fallen. No gloves, a thin jacket, pushing snow around under moonlight.

I crawled back into bed, sobbing, overwhelmed by the ways he and Lori had made our good life even better.

Jesus tells us that inviting the marginalized is important, among other reasons, because they cannot repay us (Luke 14:12–14). I see his point, but this is one area where we'll have to agree to disagree. In almost every instance, I have walked away from the full-color communion among my neighbors bearing a debt. The scales are never balanced, and the deficit is always mine.

This is the work of God, part chisel, part cannon. He'll do what it takes to demolish our "this is mine" walls. He's not even worried about it.

Only because of his unstoppable love for me did he turn my face away from myself and toward communion among the broken like me, where we share in the glory of God reflecting off each other while we plow through second helpings of cheesy vegetable soup[2] and no-brainer pork tacos.[3]

Here in the head-scratcher economy of our upside-down God, our less is always more and our fears are unwarranted. Under the canopy of a long, long life, we're surprised by the impossible goodness of surrendering our homes and discovering that as our door revolves, our souls are anchored.

When God spoke about hospitality throughout the Bible as if on a loop, he wasn't just referring to hosting a church Bible study or commiserating over steaming cups of Earl Grey with our besties.

His great hope is that we would experience the sparkling intimacy that bubbles up when we drop the veil and get real. His intention was for us to invite the stranger—the immigrant, the overlooked, the one we cannot understand, the one we say we hate—into our sanctuary and love them as we would love our own sister.

I am never closer to God than when I dare to sit next to people unafraid of telling the hard truth. The effect is contagious, and stepping toward my own brokenness is like being baptized over and over again.

Push me under—I am nothing on my own.

Pull me up—you make me new.

GROW TOGETHER

Imagine how your neighborhood would be transformed if you loved your neighbor and encouraged your children to do that too.

—*GIVE THEM GRACE*, ELYSE M. FITZPATRICK
AND JESSICA THOMPSON[1]

SOMEWHERE IN THE thick of last summer, we caught a rare, quintessential nothing-to-do sort of day. No agendas, no plans. The air was sticky; the cicadas hummed. It seemed like a bad idea not to savor it, so I grabbed my notebook to pretend like I might do some actual "work" and the novel I was reading (a more likely option) and went out to the back patio. The kids had gone missing for over an hour, and when I found them, they were sprawled throughout the playhouse, along with three of the neighbor kids, displaying various expressions of listlessness.

Entirely wordless, a few of them may have actually been on the verge of a full-on nap. The only sound was the mariachi music piped in from Silas's mini boom box, which he'd powered up with the aid of several extension cords strung across the yard.

I always know I'm truly comfortable with someone when that first long stretch of dead air hits and I don't feel the need to fill it with chatter. As I watched the languid playhouse scene unfold, it was obvious—these kids were officially friends to the end. In enduring together the specific despair of a boring, heat-shocked afternoon, they were a silently united front. It affirmed what they had known all along—we are always better together.

When we moved into our neighborhood, none of us knew a soul. The two oldest kids had sobbed over leaving their friends behind, and I wasn't sure what I could promise them in exchange. While Cory and I cautiously hung back, feeling awkward about the language barrier and hesitant to be a bother or take a risk, Calvin, Ruby, and Silas shook off their reservations and flung themselves into this new chapter without even a glance over their shoulders. Filled with the sort of carefree trust kids are famous for, they got to work, though it looked more like fun and friendship. It looked like the freedom to trust God with the details of their lives. Like most kids I know, they automatically chose the neighbor way.

Mark and Jan Foreman, authors of the exceptional parenting book *Never Say No*, describe kids as "fresh spiritual beings, not yet dulled by adult sensibilities or matter-of-fact answers. They expect to be surprised and amazed."[2] It shouldn't be such a shocker that God chooses our kids for his team as-is, not waiting until they're older, more mature, or less inclined toward bathroom humor. With the grand design of redeeming creation through neighbors who love as kin, their hearts are already half-way there. Our kids can do hard things, but before that's even possible, we've got to let them, and even encourage it. We have to fall face-first into a faith that believes the kingdom belongs equally to everyone, including people who still need help tying their shoes.

Kids are naturals at adapting and pros when it comes to drawing a wider circle. They love without judgment and serve from a place of purity. They forge friendships based on who happens to be closest. They keep on blooming. They teach us as they go.

After assuming our life would be spent sheltering our kids from anything that fell outside our lines of safety-by-way-of-uniformity, Cory and I were positioned to be knocked from our high horse yet again. It turns out, there is no minimum age requirement for stepping into the upside-down, counter-intuitive domain of Christ. My security-obsessed heart, self-conditioned for long-lane living and paralyzed by the quiet belief that folks who look and act like me are best, was unprepared for the ways God was about to shatter my false sense of control when it came to my children, proving undeniably that he was the boss all along.

Casual Dinner Convo

To say that dinnertime is a momentous occasion in my home is an understatement. Not only do I love food and eating (All food! All the eating!), cooking offers deep solace in a life that comes perilously close to screaming off the rails now and then. It's inexpensive therapy with the added perks of engaging my senses and nourishing the ones I love. It's something I can control, a problem easily solved. Crack the eggs, dice the onions, whip heavy cream into a best case scenario, invent new tacos. When life presses down on me, food is my best recourse. Give me obscure vegetation or give me death! Indeed, I used to pray that my kids would grow to love God, love reading, and not be picky eaters.

I always knew gathering together around the table would be important to my eventual family, and I daydreamed accordingly. Maybe we would hold hands when we prayed. Maybe the kids would willingly offer details about their days. Maybe we'd play one of those cute high-low conversation games.

I never imagined we'd end up talking about jail.

It comes up so often and so casually nowadays that I recently intoned, "I want you to know that not everyone goes to jail. Dad has never been to jail. I've never been to jail. You'll never go to jail . . . probably."

Our littles are moving through their formative years with a dad who works at the county jail, an older brother who was locked up for two years, and many of our favorite neighbors who have made various trips in and out of jail.

Not long ago two of Robert's friends came over for dinner. These guys, all tatted-up, with sketchy pasts, are some of the most pleasant, fun, hilarious, kindhearted young men I know. I was honored to have them at our table, and the littles, as usual, were transfixed.

Though Robert and his friends had been guests at the county jail, when I asked one of them if he had ever been to prison, a far more serious consequence than jail, he lit up and said, without an ounce of sarcasm, "Nope. Not yet!"

The "not yet" wrecked me. This doomsday mentality where a prison record is almost inevitable is a hard one to stomach. It's heartbreaking to watch. That particular night, it prompted yet another talk with the little kids once the house had cleared out.

We're often asked if our unconventional life puts our kids at risk. Do they suffer for it? Are they safe? At times, we settle for the easy answers. *Yes, of course they're safe. They don't suffer. They're never at risk.*

The longer truth is, risk swirls around us, sinister and unseen. Suffering tails us daily, not because we live in a particular neighborhood or welcome hard lives to our table, but because we are broken humans in a fallen world. It might rattle me, but I won't pull away from brokenness in some misguided effort to shield my kids from the wounded world Jesus came to save.

I'm sick to death of believing my love is earmarked only for the broken like me. *I'm more cut out for middle-class heartache, thank you very much. My solidarity is with people who think, act, talk, live like me. That goes double for my children.*

No. I have been so afraid of darkness that I've denied the darkness that sinks to the very core of myself, the wounds only grace can outrun. It took longer than I'd have liked, but I've seen too much now to deny my own dirt. If my kids are able to identify their own flaws and the reverb of grace while they're still malleable and eager to learn, I call that a win.

It took me so long to understand my purpose and find this peace, because I didn't (or wouldn't) grasp the desires of Christ. Now that I'm getting to know the God I had all along, whose heart has always beat for the low places, why wouldn't I want the same for my kids?

Five years ago I didn't realize part of my calling would be to lost boys who spend their days posturing on the streets, then land at my door and call me "Mom" after their second visit. I didn't know about these big kids, who've learned to make soup with a fistful of stones and a rusted pot. They instinctively know family and acceptance when they see it, even when they've never experienced it, and they're eager to jump in.

I never imagined I could become comfortable with any of it, much less that I would begin to see these meals as a blessing and benefit to my children, part of the mission God has for them, and not at all a risk.

It's possible that our kids are seeing more than they would have if we'd just stayed put, with our eyes on the ground directly in front of us. But God calls us to an obedience that prizes his protection over our own. He promises us gifts that leave us clinging to his grace and incomparable goodness. Rather than settling for safety and status quo, he offers us faithfulness. We don't all have to move to the city, or move to the sticks. Hallelujah, there is no one-mission-fits-all. Heartbreak, loneliness, isolation, and lack aren't organized by zip code, and he's begging all of us not to detour around the pain.

This is the unexpected road to abundance, for us and for our children.

The irony is, not only are we hesitant to allow our kids to live in the world, on mission, we're also eager to use them as prime scapegoats for our own bailout.

We miss the opportunity to reflect his glory onto people desperate to see him, because we are scared of what it might cost us or how it might change us. We take a hard but quiet stance of inaction and soothe our wrung-out consciences by telling ourselves this passivity makes us good parents. To our detriment, we make this the beginning and the end of our mission on earth. We wheel our kids out in front of any decision requiring extra faith or courage. *Nope. Sorry, Charlie. Wouldn't be good for the kids.*

We elevate our families above God's divine plan to heal humanity through his glory, but we are fooling ourselves when we believe we can rubber-stamp a guarantee of protection and provision across their lives, prioritizing their perceived safety above our call to go swiftly to hard places.

All the while, our kids wait ready to show us the way. They have so much to teach us about what it looks like to run, small and needy, to the heart of God. If we could begin to see ourselves as God sees us—children in need of his care—it just might change everything.

I'll give you an example. This past summer our three little kids headed one state away to spend a weekend with their grandparents. They have done this sort of thing without us roughly fifty times before. It's their favorite destination, sometimes because their cousins are there and always because Papaw tools them around on his golf cart and Grandma makes them pancakes every morning. Until just a few months ago, we'd never been on a family vacation, but my kids didn't even know it. "We go on vacation to Ohio!" (Kids! So dear.)

For whatever reason this particular trip presented us with some . . . obstacles. And issues. Deep, oppressive, troubling issues. The symptoms were manifest one slim hour after we dropped them off at the meeting point and went our separate ways. My mom called and quickly passed the phone to a child who shall remain nameless. I was stunned. Let's just say this kid was a few clicks away from low-grade psychosis. He/she was despondent. Despairing. Hysterical.

Cory and I soldiered on, because—*what in the world?* This

had never happened before. It was unreasonable! We knew he/ she would feel better in the morning.

What happened instead was that this "affliction" proved itself contagious, the superbug of rational, psychological well-being. Another kid dropped like a fly into the honey jar of emotional turmoil.

With copious amounts of cajoling and placating, our two little train wrecks recovered, though not to the extent that they didn't require up to seven phone calls home each day to check in.

In the end, I changed my plans and drove to their rescue a day early. When I showed up, they were kind of happy to see me, and I say that with no sarcasm. After all of their dramatic "angsting," when I came to their rescue, they registered just a slightly above normal blip of recognition and gratitude. It was sort of, "Oh, hey, Mom."

Here's what I realized. For the forty-eight hours we spent apart, I was fixated primarily on my two fragile nutcases. I missed them all—in the special way you "miss" your kids when you finally get a break from them. Miss you guys! Gotta run! I most certainly loved all three of them equally, but my mind and heart were fixed on the needy ones. I couldn't stop thinking about them, praying for them, rooting them on. My soul had drawn near to them, because they were desperate for me.

And we wonder why God allows us to stay mired in conflict, trouble, and pain. We'd really rather God draw near to us while we flit about our merry way, solving our own problems and polishing the silver. We don't want to run to him like a child. That would be silly, and we're professional adults, stouthearted and capable, with creases in our slacks. We don't want *that* kind of faith.

We want logical. Sturdy. Exemplary. It doesn't feel good to emotionally unhinge, so we keep holding it together while we steer our own ship. We know he's still with us, and some days we remember he still loves us. But we settle for a life unmarked by depth and purpose, because those things come at the cost of practicality and esteem. We adore practicality. It makes us feel so capable and smart.

Case exhibit A: I recently tried to talk Calvin out of packing his comic book Bible for our first family vacation, *because it was too heavy.* Say what? Something that should have prompted quiet thrill in my mama heart instead had me wagging my finger over convenience and common sense.

Moms (and dads!), this is what we do. We go about our important adult business, sucking all the wonder from the air with our relentless bent toward responsibility and good common sense while our kids circle us, loud, disorganized, clingy, and slightly off-balance, bearing the very secrets to entering God's kingdom.

Children have so much to teach us about what really matters and how to own our smallness, and we say no. Or not now. Or not me. Or on a good day, "Who do I make the check out to?"

We have our limits, and they usually extend to the point our hands get dirty or our neighbor looks a bit too off the grid.

When God told my family to stand right here, in this particular neighborhood of this particular city, he called all of us. He's not in the business of fragmenting families or risking some for the sake of others. We're a unit, we're all his kids, and as much as we suffer from chronic mama-bearishness, God's love for our small folks trumps ours by about 7 million percent. His fierce companionship and loyal protection puts ours straight to shame.

I want to trail blaze this world with my kids while the stakes are still relatively low. It will mean awkwardness and hard conversations we'd rather put off. It will mean staring hard at their hearts and forever weighing the tension between what feels nice and the courage and guts God called us to. It will bring us to our knees. But I believe it's worth it, and I know we're ready. We potty-trained our toddlers in the age of self-flushing toilets. We can do hard things.

If we say we trust him with our lives, we can prove it by trusting him with theirs.

Walk to School

One of the most difficult areas God asked us to trust him was with our kiddos' education. I'm using the past tense, because our fourth year in we honestly don't understand where our early fears even came from. It all feels very "Duh, of course" that they attend the low-income, once "failing" public school at the end of our street. (Don't even get me started on labeling a school in this way.)

We send our kids there just as most of our neighbors send theirs. Of course we do.

But we didn't always feel so nonchalant about it.

Though this had always been the plan, during the final weeks leading up to our move, my early resolve splintered. My nerves became a jangled mess of "what-ifs," and the chorus of skeptics didn't help. Fear barged into my heart, so I went ahead and made a bed for it. Was this anxiety actually God urging us to stay put?

Every latent worry, all of the tiny, misplaced twinges of

doubt snowballed. Change was coming, and holy cow, do we Christians prefer a wide berth around change. It makes perfect sense that I was experiencing a grab bag of emotions. That's what faith requires of us sometimes. We have to cozy up to the unknown, and our frail human selves prefer history and track records.

Of all our steps along the way, enrolling our kids in our new neighborhood's school raised the most eyebrows. We had moved from one of the most desirable districts in the state. Situated in a pristine small town, our previous school had earned its good reputation. Powered by a majority middle-class, churchgoing demographic, the school boasted test scores among the highest in the area, and things generally moved along without a hitch. In fact, kids at the elementary school still had the option of being bussed to a nearby church once a week for a Bible class during school hours. It was, and is, a top-notch school filled with good people.

To put it lightly, people struggled to compute why we would walk away.

Early into our journey, I would have been among them.

We used to think our job was to love God, follow his commands, and keep our family cloistered from the world around us. We kept our noses to the grindstone and worked at building a future where our kids would remain gated in privilege, though we never would have phrased it that way. We imagined a future for them in the stable majority. We looked around, seeing many different versions of ourselves, and believed it was the story God had penned for our family. So we jotted our own words on the page, careful not to change the script.

It took time to bring my heart to the place of accepting that maybe God's best for my kids looked different from what I had assumed. Note to self: If I ever wonder why God's plan doesn't unfold more quickly, it's because it takes me so flipping long to let go and get on board.

Over the eighteen months it took for our farm to sell, God revealed much of the junk in our hearts that insisted on our own way. There was a world waiting that we knew little about. Truth began to rattle around like a stone in our souls—the "good sense" of the world that warns us to keep our kids shielded from perceived danger—for example, kids living in poverty with parents who had the wrong kinds of tattoos and maybe even a police record—was meaningless in the eyes of God.

Logging the Gospels as proof, I'm comfortable saying that if Jesus lived on earth today as a teacher, wearing khaki pants and carrying a to-go mug of coffee, he would run to the most marginalized, maligned school in the worst neighborhood possible. He would love every kid in every single school, but he would be especially endeared to those whose low ratings for "success" were printed in red at the bottom of the list in the local newspaper. We can be confident in this, because Jesus always championed the vulnerable. The heart of God simply adores brokenness. It's his calling card, the central point behind every atom of earth and sky, and all of us here in between.

So maybe, *maybe* the little brick school at the end of our street—no bars on the windows, no security threats, no rumors of illicit drugs being peddled near the monkey bars, not the "worst" by a long shot—would be wholly acceptable after all.

Back when my concept of low-income schools was based solely on rumors and the fear-laced narrative of the media, the idea of sending my kids to one sank a cinder block in my stomach.

It's not as though I spent much time at all contemplating this scenario. It was always theoretical and hazy, but when it came to mind, I knew my kids deserved more. I believed their potential would be shortchanged. I wanted the best for them—the best facilities, the best test scores, the best programming. I suppose I wanted all kids to get a fair and sturdy education, but my priority was *my kids*, and it seemed their best shot would be at a whole-wheat, Sunday-best, middle-class, front-page, thriving elementary school.

Simply put, I saw no responsibility to try to fix anything or even to be involved. In fact, I pretended any existing inequality wasn't my problem, elevating a value that was only available or attainable for a select few.

Nicole Baker Fulgham states in her slam-dunk treatise on public education, *Educating All God's Children*, "As Christians, we are called to fix broken systems and restore what has been lost or been allowed to decay."[3]

At the moment I survey the landscape and deem something unworthy of my own kids, I am obligated to extend that sense of protectiveness to everyone else's kids. I can care about my own precious kids, but I should also care about the kids and families who don't care, or can't, or try, but fail. That is the neighbor-as-self heartbeat of the gospel.

For us, the best way to do this is to take ownership and get involved with the good work already being done on behalf of all God's children in our neighborhood.

Our beloved public school, rich with cultures, traditions, and unique opportunities for creativity and growth, is giving our kids a glimpse of heaven, where there is no foreigner, no undocumented citizen, no stranger. Only comrade. Only brother.

These are our blocks. This is our school.

We're learning to love being proven wrong.

Raising Up a You-Too Generation

It can be grueling to remain consistent when it comes to parenting. I'm the official worst, but I have my reasons. It's hard enough to uphold precisely engineered standards from the first child to the last, but throw in a twenty-one-year-old kid and I'm positively adrift. For the six months last year when we added a two-year-old to the mix, it seemed beyond the realm of all reason. We can't expect rail-straight consistency from them *or* us. I cannot oversee humans *and* charts (sticker, chore, and others). I can't dole out equal amounts of screen time with precision. I don't care who said what first, and when it comes to hygiene, I default to optimistically hands-off. There are simply too many people, representing too many quirks and personality shortcomings!

I'm better with broad issues, worldview kinds of things.

Living as an inclusive, wide-circle, *you-too* family is important to Cory and me. We talk about it often with our kids, in ways that are both natural (parenting win!) and forced (*sigh*). It's usually hard to say whether they actually hear us. Typically, Calvin is more concerned with finagling extra Minecraft time, Ruby is gluing trash into the form of a makeshift dollhouse, and Silas is squirreling away all the empty containers he can scavenge while we're distracted by our own yammering.

They're very normal, amply personalitied, often-fighty and disagreeable, funny and spunky kids. No halos here! Just keep walking.

Now and then we catch a tiny glimmer that shows they're

getting it, but when Ruby gave all her Barbies to the girls up the street, it felt like taking things too far. After all, we had bought those Barbie dolls for her. They were gifts. She would miss them! Besides, it wasn't right of the girls to ask for them. *We will not enable shaky etiquette.*

The excuses flew from my mouth as the Holy Spirit filled my heart. *Let her learn to love giving. Teach her to hold loosely to stuff and surrender with love. Lead her in generosity. Show her it's not up to us to decide who qualifies as "deserving."*

She has never missed those fool Barbies. Not once has she lamented her decision or felt entitled to replacements.

Left to my instincts, I get overprotective about all the wrong things. I settle for scarcity instead of abundance. I think about words like *unfair.* See what happens when humans are left to raise other humans? Are you catching on to just how far I still have to go? I nearly forfeited the freedom of living open-handed for a few buxom pieces of plastic.

Graciously, God keeps calling us back to him, the moms along with the little children, the neighbors and friends. He draws us near and we grow together.

Trail Blazing

My mom is a practical woman. She's kind but not fussy. She mothered my brother, sister, and me to think for ourselves and held more faith in us than was perhaps warranted. She epitomized the concept of free-range parenting, picked the right battles, and, for my kindergarten "Tasting of the Green" bash, introduced my classmates and me to kiwifruit, no easy feat considering our rural, quasi-food-desert situation.

During a time in my elementary years when I battled night-time fear and insomnia, she never told me to say the alphabet backward or even to pray, or if she did, it's not what I remember. What I remember are two distinct nights, the first when she said, "When I can't sleep, I imagine I'm living back on the frontier, like Laura Ingalls. I pretend it's time to push west and think hard about everything we need for the journey. Then I load the wagon." (The woman is a glaring creative, and she refuses to accept it!)

Then, on another night, "When I can't sleep, I pretend I have a bunch of extra money, and I think about who I would give it to."

If I tell you my childhood was nearly perfect, that my dad was the favorite chaperone for all our class trips and my mom had a way of spinning magic from the meager, I'm leaving much of the story unsaid. First, the concept of extra money would have been entirely foreign. I overheard so many discussions of "making ends meet" that my kid brain twisted it into "endsmeat," the direst, most lonely dinner option known to man. *Crud. We can't even make endsmeat.*

I'm also not talking about the number of hours I watched TV (quite a few) or the dinners served with love from a box. If you asked, it wouldn't cross my mind to delve into my dad's long hours working away from our home and how that shaped us. I'd forget about the times we made each other cry or (even worse) retreat.

I'd tell you it was nearly perfect because it was, and it might have had something to do with the fact that my mom said, "I think about who I would give it to," not, "I think about what I would buy."

When I consider the responsibility of raising up little ones (kids we parent, kids we live near, kids at church—we're all parents in one way or another), my gut says the only way to pass down the things that matter in life is by living them. If we're desperate to not perpetuate lies about name brands and popular toys, our kids need to see us not caring about what's "cool" or accumulating unnecessary things. If we know their longings won't ever be filled by chasing what sparkles, we'd better keep space for things the world calls dim. And if we want them to love their neighbor as much as they love themselves, we need to show them the way.

We can give our children *that*, friends. We can.

We can't always say yes. We can't anticipate and deflect all their hurts. We can't cook them organic meals every night at six or hang fringed Pottery Barn Kids curtains from their windows. We can't answer every question or plan a weekly craft day. We can't provide a constant stream of entertainment or even consistent family devotions. We will lose our tempers and sometimes be moody and mean. We cannot begin to teach them enough about God or grace, and we sure can't decide eternity for them. But we can guide them along the path of generosity rather than greed. We can walk in a way that gets loud and rowdy about real treasure.

We can plainly, imperfectly, live what we say we believe.

We can humble ourselves and learn from their pure hearts and gusto.

We can offer them the freedom to fall to small places, where God's glory and goodness bounce around the room and they see for themselves—*this* is who God is. *This* is how he loves me.

9

COMMUNE

Unless churches today can recover a sense of parish responsibility, of belonging to people and place, we will continue to propagate the disembodied Christianity.

—SLOW CHURCH, C. CHRISTOPHER
SMITH AND JOHN PATTISON[1]

I WAS BORN into a church with worn burgundy carpeting, an Awana program for kids on Wednesday evenings, and a tightly knit community of farmers, secretaries, teachers, and carpenters. My parents gathered with their friends after evening church, cackling over Bible Trivia too late on school nights, their hands salty in the popcorn bowl. Church became an extension of who I was and who I am now. Its halls paved a way for me to be known among the ordinary. I still remember its smell.

But nothing good stays untouched for long. We eventually moved on.

My heritage was built on long wooden benches, women in bonnets on one side, long-bearded men on the other. Finely woven into my faith are fibers of Sunday mass: stand, kneel, wait in line. I watched from a distance as aunts and cousins took the wafer and imagined its shape in my Protestant mouth.

There were quiet, nondescript churches where I sat undetected for months, eventually walking away without having ever been seen. I've observed God as a pop song, God as a judge. I have beheld prayer coverings and prayer flags. I've seen men dance the aisles and women fall to the floor, their legs modestly covered with a white sheet until the Spirit waned and they were ready to rise.

In just shy of forty years, I've worshipped in hand-carved cathedrals, highbrow sanctuaries, dank gymnasiums, and open-air pavilions.

I have seen it all, heard it all.

Yet across decades of vacation Bible school, youth group, Christian college, and consistent Sunday attendance, I knew shockingly little about what church was intended to be. I knew it was something I was supposed to do.

But none of it made me free.

Along the way, I tasted enough truth to make me hungrier. My parents and others around us, upheld by their resolute faith through financial crises, illness, family turmoil, grief, loss, and the intermittent pain of ordinary life, were sugar on my tongue. As a teenager I was welcomed as a stranger into a close body of believers, receiving their support and encouragement as the very grip of grace. These secondhand truths sank down to my roots, carrying me through years where doubt was a boomerang and my faith had grown stale, quietly sustaining me through seasons where my soul was choked with drought.

All the while God's presence was around me, a raging

undertow. He was the air I breathed, the gravity that held me in place. When my fickle heart loved the wrong thing, he pulled from the other side. My life as a Christian was equal parts yank and shove. Would I ever get it right? Would I ever care enough? Not a day passed that I didn't trace his shape somewhere against my foggy horizon. But by most accounts I did my faith all wrong.

I loved him. I always did.

I just wasn't sure about his church.

Walking to Church

Soon after settling in to our new community, my family wandered into a tiny congregation at the end of our street and found ourselves strangely at home. It wasn't its size or programming that impressed us. We didn't know a soul inside its walls and hadn't heard a bit of buzz around town. It had nothing to do with the facilities, the sound system, or the hype of the children's ministry. Quite honestly, we weren't initially sure what it was that drew us in. But what we thought was just a courtesy visit, checking in by default because it was only a block away and we'd failed the night before to line up a "real" contender, ended up answering a question we hadn't even known to ask.

With the sun streaming through the stained glass and my bony back settling in against the pew, I found the palpable, undeniable presence of the Holy Spirit between pops of the failing sound system and arms that welcomed me, again, as a stranger.

It wasn't supposed to happen this way. I wasn't even a Methodist, for Pete's sake.

One by one, my bad ideas about what mattered began to fall away. As each one hit the worn-down carpet, the axis of my soul tilted, and I remembered that down is up in the kingdom of heaven. Little is much. God isn't surprised by our imperfections or disappointed when we worship slightly off-key. In fact, against the backdrop of his improbable kingdom, our humblest offerings are always the sweetest.

This is the church that would teach us about roots and the beauty of showing up not to be entertained or spoon-fed, but to commune with the Holy Spirit and roll up our sleeves to serve our community in practical, humble ways. The people inside its walls would heal us and break our hearts. And God wouldn't waste a single second. Traversing the rubble that's sure to exist as long as people do, he would continue to point us back to himself, inviting us to be stayers in a world looking over its shoulder, ever ready to bolt.

Church has become a complicated beast for many of us. Our buildings swell as our body shrinks. On a good day, we wonder what it would take to change things and why it's often such a struggle to care. On our worst days, we don't even bother with the questions.

I will now state the obvious: I am not a theologian. Nor am I a historian of the Christian church. Denominational differences typically leave me somewhere between befuddled and flat bored. I can't keep them straight, and I don't know why most of them matter.

None of these qualifiers has stopped me from dispensing more than my fair share of grumbling over the years, detailing the myriad ways churches have failed to please me.

The music was too slow. Too loud. Too old-school. Too popular. Too produced.

The kids' program was disorganized. Too much candy.

Not enough structure. Too fun. Just call me your modern-day Jonathan Edwards.

The ladies at Bible study didn't "get" me. And by the way, I wouldn't have chosen the book we were reading, but naturally, no one asked me.

Too much grace, too much brimstone, etc., etc., etc.

Without even catching my mistake, I had idealized "church" into a temple created to fit perfectly around the shape of my precious soul. I was fine. I was great. I wasn't looking to be changed by the communion of its fellowship. I clearly wasn't searching for Jesus.

The Spirit of God doesn't accept invitations according to who throws the best parties. If I'd have wrenched my eyes off myself for even a second, I wouldn't have had to look twice for him. "For where two or three gather together as my followers, I am there among them" (Matt. 18:20). Once I had him in my sights, you'd have had to pry me off the pew.

Surrounded by a sea of white curls in our new haphazard, multigenerational, semiliturgical church, I began to consider that I'd been pointing my finger in the wrong direction all along. The problem, at its soggy root, had always been me.

Quite by accident I was on a path of discovering what actually matters when it comes to church.

Before I Go

Now and then I have to leave my home overnight. I speak sometimes at conferences or churches, and though I limit my time away, it never fails to throw all my people into a tizzy. Everyone freaks out. Especially me.

It's not this way when, um, *other* people leave for a night or two.

And now, a quick round of compare and contrast.

Cory hasn't had to travel for business since he worked in politics, but the last time he headed out on a two-day trip, he packed a quick bag consisting of two dress shirts (ironed by *moi*), twelve white T-shirts (no time for counting!), zero socks (details, details), and a toothbrush. On his way out the door, he kissed us all good-bye, leaving the kids with the vague impression that he'd be back around five thirty for dinner, as usual.

I recently had a two-dayer, and here's how mine went down. Before I could pack, I first needed to do laundry. While I was in the zone, I figured I might as well do all of it. I stocked the fridge, signed two permission slips, and shoved errant library books into backpacks. I also cubed a cantaloupe, fashioned Ruby's hair into a cute style that would withstand the winds of my absence, and made myself a snack for the road. Then I detailed a complex schedule of events, after-school activities, and overall expectations that would rival the daily itinerary of the United States president.

Listen: dads are amazing. I'm weak-kneed with gratitude every time Cory handles the paperwork related to insurance, accounts, or general gobbledygook. The fact that he scrubs the burners when I (always, every time) boil over the milk and cleans out all the clogged drains might be the sexiest qualities I never knew to imagine. I'll just put it out there like it's no big deal: I have never once mowed our yard. It's shameful, yes, but only until I remember how awesome it is to have a hard-working, capable husband. At that point, I'm just profoundly grateful.

But since I'm the boss of our inside operations, my absence is never without its share of cluster headaches. And I'm usually only going to Kansas.

When Jesus began quietly planning in earnest for his departure *from planet Earth*, I'm sure it was obvious that so many ducks were so out of whack. We couldn't be left to figure stuff out for ourselves. It was time for him to start speaking plainly about the church he would leave behind and his plans for her.

Spoiler alert: that church is us. We're it. Doesn't that seem like a bad idea, to leave his great name in our hands? Wouldn't it have been nice if, when he spoke about his dreams for his church, he was referring to optimal sermon length and parish care instead?

His plan was for us to gather in purposeful community, grow with intention, and experience the power of worshipping alongside one another. Perhaps we would go about these meaningful rites in a space we inexplicably, lacking a single ounce of inventiveness, defined as "church." But make no mistake, by God's design and Jesus' decree, church was never about buildings, budgets, or bylaws. It was always about us and his plans for our redemption.

As his crucifixion neared, he wasn't busy making lists about who would clean the temple or how often. He was gathering his flock and finding a lay-shepherd. Per usual, when it came time to roll out the nuts and bolts of the operation, he turned away from the religious elite, looked straight in the eyes of a man who was among the most spiritually disheveled, and simply said, "You."

Just before predicting his death, Jesus asked his twelve the famous question, "Who do you say I am?" and Simon, quick to impress, had an answer. "You are the Messiah, the Son of the living God."

Jesus replied, "You are blessed, Simon son of John, because my Father in heaven has revealed this to you. You did not learn this from any human being. Now I say to you that you are Peter (which means 'rock'), and upon this rock I will build my church" (Matt. 16:17–18).

There's plenty of dispute over exactly what Jesus meant here (missing the forest for the trees—a hallmark of the Christian faith!), but what we can surely agree on is that when it came time for Jesus to begin building his church, he used as his primary example an imperfect person whose history in the faith had often tracked a jagged path.

Simon was a complicated bundle of conflicting personality quirks. His passions caused him grief, and his flaws might as well have been a sign around his neck pointing out his chronic inability to manage himself. He was fiery, opinionated, stubborn, impulsive, reckless, fickle, and judgmental. He was a bit of a busybody, prone to worrying about others when he would have been wise to train a steadier eye on himself. On top of that was his strong bent toward saving face no matter what and his obsession with maintaining popularity among the cool kids.

He was basically Shannan Martin, only probably hairier and more proficient in the ways of catching dinner.

Jesus, equal parts buzz-worthy and polarizing, knew what it meant to surround himself well. He knew everything about everyone, saw each person for what he or she actually was, *in him*, not just what the person appeared to be on paper. Of all his beloved disciples, he chose Simon extra hard, shuttling him right into his inner circle, along with John and James.

Unschooled and ordinary, Simon had the faith—and attention span—of a child. He was apt to take his eyes off Jesus, particularly right after he'd seen proof of his power. He was passionate, all-in, quick to forget, and painfully human.

He didn't trick Jesus or try to hide his worst. Jesus knew he would deny him, but whatever. It didn't matter in light of his mad love for Simon. He saw in him all the raw materials it would take to show the rest of us some fundamentally important things, like his deep love for his people, the way he stood ready to forgive, his knack for calling the unqualified, and his inclination to create space for the small and unspectacular.

Just like you and me, Jesus saw Simon as a sinner in desperate, continual need for him and said, "Yes. He's just who I want." When he gave Simon a new name—Peter, "the Rock"—it was a promise for all of us, but also a warning. God's church was created to reflect his glory, and his glory happens to be soaked to its tips in acceptance and mercy. None of us stands without him.

Peel back our put-on churchy manners, and you'll see the truth: we'd like our houses of God to be sanitary places of worship rather than shabby hostels stacked with weary travelers. We don't really want obvious sinners in our neat rows of cushioned chairs, or we'll tolerate them only long enough for them to pull themselves together and become like the rest of us. We certainly don't want to be Simon. We prefer to believe we've learned from him without actually being him. We want to skip right over the Simon years and just be Peter 2.0, all rock, no mud.

In Simon, we see ourselves as we are, doubting, overeager, judgmental, and ungracious. And in Simon we also see the unexpected plan of God over our lives, where without our failures we cannot taste the freedom of being bought. Look closely. Stare hard. Do you believe Jesus wants to shape our Simon-ness into a solid body of humble, teachable Peter people? Do you trust that he can, and that we're worthy only because he says so?

Under the gaze of Christ, Simon becomes Peter, and God's church is built with men and women whose only hope is that we might be a bit less faithless tomorrow than we were today.

●　■　❧

A couple of months ago I attended the first annual Jail Ministry banquet for the county jail where Cory is chaplain. I wouldn't have missed it for the world, and the oversized wedges of Amish-baked pie had only a little to do with it.

I'm at a stage of life where I've come to a jarring and profound understanding of my personal soft spots. Along with taking communion, watching kids try their best at hard things, and that scene in *Walk the Line* where June Cash levels Johnny with grace, watching Cory do his job happens to be one of the things that gets me right in the gut. I never imagined that college kid with a ball cap pulled down over his longish hair and an earring would one day shepherd misfits.

I'd swiped on waterproof mascara, knowing Cory would have plenty to say about his friends and the ways they continue to teach him about an abundant life. But I had no clue that I'd walk away that night with a clearer picture of what church was meant to be, thanks to the simple, honest words of a man getting his first taste of true freedom.

I didn't know a guy named Doug would cause me to choke back sobs.

He stood shy at the microphone, in blue jeans and a nice

shirt, sharing quietly about all he'd lost from the bottle and a lifetime of being dragged behind the wagon. His was a story of desperation and raw humanity. It might have been easy to look out across a crowd of dressed-up church folks and sugarcoat it. I wouldn't have blamed him a bit if he'd left some things out. But I'm glad he didn't.

When Doug found himself back in jail for the fifth time, any hope he'd ever held evaporated into the air around him. He resigned himself to a purposeless life and a sure death.

In a testament of his relentless pursuit of Doug, God was already at work, orchestrating the rescue that would come from the fall. With nothing in common but a string of legal entanglements and a propensity to make a hard life even harder, his bunkmate, James, was a most unlikely messenger of love. Looking him square in his bloodshot eyes, James spoke the words that would alter Doug's future. "You're at rock bottom? You got nothing left to lose? Well, the good news is, that's right where God wants you."

Those words broke Doug. Sometimes freedom is a hairline crack in a cinder block, just enough for light to spill into the cell we're in. Sometimes, the only key that will fit the lock is someone else's willingness to meet us at our worst and tell us the truth.

Doug's voice cracked when he spoke onstage about that night in his cell. And I had to willfully hold myself back from the ugly cry.

His story wasn't even half-told.

With his heart freshly split to receive grace and love, Doug began receiving visits from a man in his seventies, who faithfully showed up to speak truth across the crackling jailhouse video phone and into the torn-up life of a stranger. The Word he'd been reading said to visit lost souls in their distress, track them down, find them on their worst days, and make room for them at the table. So he did.

Back when criminals were only theoretical in my life, or viewed from the safe distance of my TV screen, I saw jail as a threat, a punishment. There was no room in my rigid worldview for an entire sector of God's children who find him at the lowest point of their lives and get the shakes when they consider facing the outside world again. I'd never considered that liberty could sink lead into the gut of institutionalized people who have been taught to fear themselves.

When Doug began to bear the weight of his freedom, he knew where to turn. He ran straight to his friend, finding a secure home inside a church committed to walking beside him.

He didn't care if their worship services were traditional or contemporary. He wasn't concerned about the color of the carpeting or which Bible translation they read. He had no preferences when it came to denomination or church bylaws. It didn't matter to him whether or not the music was cool, or if the coffee they served met his standards of excellence. It was of no consequence if the pastor wore a necktie or a shirt that snapped all the way up.

Doug went because he was welcomed among a congregation of equally wounded believers who weren't afraid of seeing themselves in his weary face. They took seriously their job description to be a refuge for the wounded, not because it was a task required of them, but because their own redemption depended on it, and their love compelled them.

When I was a little girl, someone asked me how many people I had saved. He said he had saved six, but his dad was up somewhere in the twenties. Even with plastic bird barrettes clipped to my hair and Velcro tennis shoes on my feet, the claim struck me as bogus. Making disciples is far more than leading a "sinner" in a prayer, walking away, and carving a tally mark onto a pew.

Without God dropping us low enough to lose ourselves in a trade for more of him, our hearts will not begin to match the beating of his for the poor and marginalized. In order to care, we have to find ourselves in the lines on their faces. And once we do, we'll see it as mandatory to go to them and share their pain.

This is the long road to discipleship, and the understanding that our own discipleship doesn't end once we're pulled up dripping from baptismal water. It will require a commitment toward the uncomfortable, acquiring the sort of grit that refuses to give up. Anything else means we're content to continue snacking on the status quo of our pretty lives and our tired faith. We're not so pretty after all, and we sure aren't free.

Quite bluntly, we have lost our way. Rather than being reclaimed by the alliance of our poverty, we've learned to endure a false community of the proud polite. We've sworn membership to our feel-good Sunday club where the real troublemakers are outside our walls, and we're honestly a bit suspicious when one straggles in. We maintain the illusion of "family" despite not even truly knowing one another. But hey, that's what boundaries are for—separation of church and life and all that jazz.

There's something profoundly true and even beautiful about the phrase "seeker friendly," but we've forgotten that the only thing seekers—including our ever-wandering, always-seeking selves—are searching for is God. Seekers aren't sniffing around for a better light show or a more perfectly delivered homily or even an hour of free child care. They might think they're looking for belonging or new friends or a sure road toward a better life, but what they simply don't know yet is that God's unquenchable love for them is at the root of all good things.

To our detriment, we've swallowed the hook that says a good church is hip, wired, programmed to the hilt, and offers a top-notch coffee bar. With intentions that might actually be good, we wring the gospel from our meetings and are left with something that might appeal to members of a certain social status (rags in the eyes of God) but scarcely resembles Jesus. We try to be all things to all people, then sit back in frustration, wondering why we've become a congregation of spoiled people who can't get along.

We applaud perfection and choreograph redemption, inadvertently creating a hierarchy of belonging on the rungs of which true community perishes.

We sing "come as you are" from our hymnals and PowerPoint slide shows while doing everything in our power to define ourselves as cool, not stopping to consider how this might alienate ordinary folks with complicated stories. We hold fast to the tenets of our middle-class theology, elevating ourselves as good and exemplary, denying that this is not the essence of who we are.

Our double standard is blinding.

Talk to a man like Doug, tears tracked with profound gratitude, and you will find it impossible to believe that church was ever meant to be anything but a halfway house. Without lost and torn-up people, our churches become museums with admission fees and glass cases, rather than twenty-four-hour emergency clinics. And without cracks of our own, we cannot absorb the pain of another.

When Doug stood wobbly kneed on the stage, sober for the longest stretch of his adult life, it was because there were men in his life who looked at him and saw themselves. They reflected God's glory by offering their kinship.

Had I visited Doug's church, I'm certain it wouldn't have met my demands. It's humble and probably bears our twenty-first-century, kiss-of-death descriptor—"old-school." I so often forget it's the slow, quiet, often thankless and largely unnoticed work of the gospel that God esteems.

If we could try to remember this, and live as though it's true, maybe marriages wouldn't end and addictions wouldn't spiral out of control, hiding in the dark, scared of being found out.

Maybe rather than being a standard no one can meet, church could become a soft place for all of us to fall.

Freedom comes at the cost of vulnerability. This is where we've failed the hardest. There's more than enough blame to go around.

I know we can all do better. There isn't one way of doing church that is holier than another. I have seen both large and tiny congregations willing to surrender nonessentials in order to walk in their calling. A church committed to its immediate neighborhood with laser focus is one who understands the gospel of generosity and service, and there are no parameters excluding a body from obedience to this holy work.

But. Our cities and neighborhoods are teeming with neglected and abandoned congregations trying to pool their resources in order to love the Dougs among us into the fold. They probably aren't doing church precisely the way we might prefer, but they need us. And we need them. The humble, neighborhood church is an unlikely powerhouse we've trained our eyes to overlook.

Like the traditional concept of church parishes, many of us

live within a few miles—or even within walking distance—from an imperfect body of Christ followers doing their best to impact the place of their jurisdiction.

What would it look like if more of us set aside our tired preferences and grabbed hands with them? How would our neighborhoods change if we committed to worshipping and serving together? Claiming a place for the long haul is a powerful reminder of our commitment to slow growth and a culture of with-ness that can only saturate its community over time with a near-stubborn faithfulness. We are essentially adopting the church as our own, or even accepting it as an extension of ourselves. We are for this body, because we are here with it. We will do all we can to ensure loyalty to its mission.

Without being rooted to place, everything else becomes up for grabs. Though it is imperative that the holy Word of God reign in it, our other gripes and complaints are revealed as picky preferences, an inability to accept imperfection and, by default, our unwillingness to acknowledge that we are just as flawed. Juxtaposed against a faith that has never cost us a thing, might we be willing to surrender our wish list and let our roots take hold wherever God has planted us? Could we begin to truly believe the Holy Spirit is vibrant and alive wherever two or more are gathered together in his name, no bells or whistles required? Could we simply *be* the church we long for?

Smoke Break

I could write line after line in an attempt to show you how God used an unassuming church with its faltering technologies and half-empty pews to move our hearts into the space where they were meant to beat. I could talk about the sermons and the way they unfurled in my soul like the petals of a late-blooming rose. I could share how I was challenged to confront a new presence of God that was every bit as alive in a prewritten prayer and a Celtic blessing as he had been in the haphazard, freewheeling, tambourine-banging church of my youth.

I could talk about all those things, and you might begin to understand.

Or, I could just tell you about the smokers.

Sometime during our first year at our new church, I had run home after the service to grab my side dish for the carry-in lunch.

Pulling back into the lot ten minutes later, I noticed an intriguing congregation of men on the north side of the building. There were a few guys around my age, and a few a little older, some I knew well and a couple I only recognized. One hid a Cubs T-shirt under his burgundy choir robe, a cigarette dangling from his tenor lips. A quiet group of loyal servants and leaders of our church had gathered there, and all of them were smoking.

From my van, I raised my eyebrows and grinned. "What's going on over there?"

"Oh, nothing good," one of them sheepishly smiled back, snuffing out his cigarette and walking my way. "Need a hand?"

I loaded him up with pickles and beans.

And I knew for the hundredth time that I was home.

It's not because our church is perfect, not because it's everything I always thought a church home should be, not because everyone gets along and behaves graciously, or because it meets all my piddly needs. In the past year there have been arguments and even heartbreaking divisions. At turns we have wavered on the fence along with others. *Should we leave?*

But week after week we run out the door five minutes late, walk down the back alley, and take our seat among a community of stouthearted misfits who aren't afraid to straight-up wear their humanity, even on a Sunday.

These are people who can handle my scars and whatever battle wounds lay ahead of me. I am free to struggle beside them and even to voice my doubts.

The kind welcome they extend humbles us into admitting that our assumptions might have been wrong. But it's the smokers who showed us our place at the table.

Yes, they could have waited until they got home.

They could have taken pains to relocate to a more obscure location.

All that would have accomplished among the rest of us is the mounting dread that everyone is better at this holiness gig and the looming despair that what's required of us is either to be "good" or to pull up our pantyhose and at least act the part.

Broken for Me

On the first Sunday of each month, we file up to the altar to receive communion. Though not a foreign concept to me, communion had never been so frequent in my past. At first, once a month seemed like overkill.

I used to think the power communion held was primarily over my mind. *Look what Jesus did for me.* Body and blood, I received them, guilty over the ways I walked away feeling the same, wondering all over again what was wrong with me.

Our first fall as part of the congregation turned to winter, then spring. The air around us did its dance as tulips pushed their newborn lips through the cold earth and we all exhaled together. At every stop along the way, through ice and sun and the smoke of burning leaves, our hearts were anchored by the bread and the cup.

The circle of life is echoed in the wide returning of a soul to its maker. I am from dust, and to dust I will return. Dirt to dirt, I was made to live low. *Remember this.*

It didn't take long to find myself longing for the first Sunday of the month. It always arrived well past time. My soul needed to fall to its knees.

One particular Sunday, it wasn't our pastor who served the holy meal.

A pair of teenagers stood at the front of the church, each holding half a loaf of bread and a goblet of grape juice, the same two kids I'd seen walking up the alley the day before with their arms entangled and the whole world bearing down on their backs. Two lines of congregants formed, one for each of them. I stood before the girl, who looked me dead in the eye and mumbled, "Christ's body, broken for you." Her hair was wild, and I knew she was living one thousand different hurts. She had wounded and *was* wounded. Just like me. I saw my own pain in their faces and was overcome by the urge to grab hold of them both, suddenly understanding our chances of making it to shore were so much better if we treaded water together.

I swallowed down all the grace, all the life, all of my salvation, and it never made more sense. Our voices rose together, a mash-up of different lives, different worldviews, different generations, different-colored collars. It didn't even matter a little. "If you tarry till you're better, you will never come at all."[2]

These days, the bread sticks a bit on its way down. It's never easy anymore. The old girl inside me, the one fighting to believe any good thing should be simple, worries I'm not doing something right. It used to slide right down without costing me a thing.

I've never been more aware of the mess I am. I can't outrun my humanity, and I'm done trying. I need this practice, this bending low to confess my simpleminded heart. I need the routine wonder of offering my infant gratitude to the one who defragments my humanity into what it really is, a pulsing brokenness, a needle skipping in the groove of imperfection and frailty.

Up at the altar, two men standing shoulder to shoulder swallowed their own pride along with the bread. One wore the tips of angels' wings etched across his shaved head, fresh from prison, tied in knots over all he stood to lose. The other was an officer of the law.

Held to the light of the body and the blood, there are simply no boundaries separating us. The difference between those two men was but a vapor of Christ. In his death, they are both made whole. In what was spilled, they can be full.

The same goes for the rest of us.

In a tiny church, half-empty, where women shuffle in with tattooed chests and the homeless guy across town shows up wearing the essence of yesterday's buzz, the focus locks in place. Life makes more sense after wedging a soggy hunk of bread into my cheek and whispering truth as I exhale—*You did this for me. Please don't let me forget. Please keep coming for me.*

I know the power of that jagged tear of bakery bread. I know the promise of the cup.

It lives inside us, pushing past our faithless hearts, our vanity and pride, our ruthless refusals to get cozy with our own splintered souls.

We can either masquerade as capable earners or fall needy into the arms of a Savior who makes us free. There is no space within our souls to do both.

Among the company of misfits, in the shared cup, in the midst of our unfair judgments and staggering arrogance, God reels our hearts back to him.

We are feeble. Flawed. Quick with a hug.

We're clinging. Sometimes questioning.

We are beggars.

And this is the astounding kingdom of heaven that won't ever stop surprising us.

10

GIVE MORE

Generous: Showing a readiness to give more of something, as money or time, than is strictly necessary or expected.
—Oxford Pocket Dictionary of Current English[1]

IT WASN'T LONG after Robert moved in for the first time that we began to get a clear understanding of who he really is.

Everyone warned us it would happen.

As an advocate for mentoring, I know walking with a tough-guy teenager prone to putting his fist through walls is a beautiful concept. But as important and transforming as it can be, mentoring is still somewhat safe. At the end of the day, everyone goes back to their respective corners until next time. Mentoring might have jarred our perspective a bit, but it couldn't have prepared us to move that same young man into the basement and call him our son.

We had no idea what we were signing up for.

The first month was the hardest. I knew we were in over our

heads when a cell phone flew across the room and hit the wall. I had a feeling things might get ugly; I just never imagined I would be the one throwing things.

The true colors were coming out. Though we'd known Robert for several years, it had been somewhat from the periphery. Now he was living in our little house with a tracking device locked around his ankle, not even allowed to step off our front steps except to go to work.

My patience was being stretched so thin it became transparent in the middle. We were being distilled down to our truest states. And we learned a few things about our tallest kid.

Most obvious was his humor and bent toward affection, along with his reckless, unfounded optimism. A brazen extrovert, he likes to stay near the action. He's got a soft spot for ketchup and a massive crush on Taylor Swift (!!!).

He's also the most generous person I've ever met.

Ask any of our kids how often we talk about generosity, and they'll tell you we never shut up about it. The waters got muddy pretty quickly as we watched Robert manage a steady factory job with a meager paycheck and a friend group that ensured a constant stream of "opportunities" to share.

On our watch he wired money to long-lost relatives, bought train tickets for prodigal sisters, helped support kids he hadn't fathered (along with those he had), and held the carte blanche prerogative that if his "brother" (not his brother!) Fernando asked for anything, he would always hand it over. Always.

Our response was usually to harp on him about not giving his money away, even saying things like, "You need to worry about yourself first." In those moments, what we said we believed no longer held water. *This was different.* We slid right back to the place we thought we'd climbed out of. Watching him navigate life and ownership messed with all our ideas. Separating ourselves into our middle-class column, we left him on the other side and told ourselves the gospel meant different things for different people.

I was challenged by his easy (too easy!), wider-circle (too wide!) view of family. Though I said his approach was my end goal, I launched into a skeptical game of semantics whenever he referred to someone as his cousin or sister. His loose grip on his possessions made me fret about his future. Quietly, subtly, I regarded him as a "them," quick to forget God created us all simply as his.

Each afternoon I chatted across the kitchen island with a really tall, "really ripped" (his words) young guy inked up with DIY tattoos, with hair in various states of "did." I was prepared for anger mismanagement and gripes about the house rules. I was right that he'd be distant and sullen sometimes, and that he'd complain about my cooking.

I never expected my newest son, with all his bad habits and his complicated, questioning faith, to show me so much about the heart of Jesus.

My hypocrisy made me squirm.

❦ ❦ ❦

A few years back, when God's words about my responsibility to love my neighbor and care for the poor shot through me like a thousand watts, I was overcome. Like a blind man finally able to see, I felt as if everything around me was new, and it left me with a sensory migraine. I was stunned by the glaring need I'd glossed over for so long.

Funny thing is, I'd always thought of myself as a generous person.

I was raised to hold things loosely and share what I had. When I saw a need, I often responded. But I was largely oblivious to the disparity between my excess and the lack that throbbed around me like a bruise. I gave what was asked of me, tithing my 10 percent because to do otherwise felt like the Christian version of bad karma. Now and then I even gave extra. But I never really sacrificed.

I shushed my conscience, reminding myself that though I had more than enough, it could be worse.

Oh, it got worse. Just not in the way I'd expected.

As I began to read with my new set of eyes, the Bible took on a decided lean toward sacrifice. The foundation of my faith no longer looked incidental or benign.

Right around the time Jesus was beginning his earthly ministry, resident wild-child John the Baptist was sent by God along the banks of the Jordan River, baptizing people into the family of God. We're already aware that John teetered on the line between bold and slightly bonkers. His words to the crowds, as retold in Luke 3, leave no room for dispute. The dude was straight up antiestablishment. He didn't care about appealing to the masses, he wasn't trying to make God fit the existing paradigm, and he wasn't interested in leaving people with the impression that pursuing righteousness was without a distinct, personal cost. (It's obvious they didn't have youth group in John's day, as he may have benefited from some evangelism role play.)

To set the mood, as crowds lined up to be baptized, John called them a "brood of snakes" (v. 7). He bossed them up one side and down the other about the ways they'd screwed everything up, then called them on things they hadn't even gotten the chance to say out loud.

Forget about a tender closing. He skipped over the classic "every eye closed, every head bowed, no one looking around" bit and wrapped it up with this zinger: "Even now the ax of God's judgment is poised, ready to sever the roots of the trees. Yes, every tree that does not produce good fruit will be chopped down and thrown into the fire" (v. 9). Bear in mind, John wasn't witnessing at a Hell's Angels rally or even responding to naysayers. He was speaking to a long line of people who had shown up because they knew, on some level, that their spirits were poor.

Taking in his holy fury, swallowing down the brimstone because they hungered for truth, the people asked the question that will tail me and the rest of humanity until we're all swept up into glory: "What should we do?" (v. 10).

I mean, seriously, John. *Tell us what to do.* We are dreamers and believers, but we're also ready to do the work and live like we mean it. Pull us up from the water; we want to be changed. We're just not always sure how that should look.

Here's a list of things John did *not* tell them to do: memorize more Scripture, pray on your knees in the morning instead of in bed and half-asleep, get up in time to make it to Sunday school, wear shorts that cover your knees, only watch PG-rated movies, quit smoking, and, for the love, keep your hair off your collar.

Here's what he did say: "If you have two shirts, give one to the poor. If you have food, share it with those who are hungry" (v. 11). "Don't take more than you need." Be content.

The good news doesn't begin with control, but surrender.

I was thunderstruck. The line about the two shirts hit particularly close to home, considering I'd once posted a picture on my blog of my six, nearly identical, blue and white pinstriped button-downs. Never mind the rest of my closet. Lalalalala! There's no story here!

When God woke us up to the ways we were neglecting our mission to knit generosity into the fabric of our everyday lives, my personality, which functions from largely opposing poles, rocketed from sweeping denial, "A good God would never ask me to do this impossible thing!" to overzealous, hyperdrive obedience, where I wanted to rip everything off the walls and send it up in a holy plume of smoke. It was too much. It hurt to look around and see all our stuff. I wanted it gone. The thrift-store paintings? Kindling. The quilts and extra sets of sheets, the ten pairs of shoes, the dishes I only used twice a year? If I could have snapped my fingers and rendered them dust, I would have.

My menagerie of pretty things closed in like a band around my chest. It was an ecclesiastic paradigm shift for the ages, but without the eating and drinking and general *"what the hey!"* merriment. Everything suddenly felt meaningless.

In light of Jesus' instruction to his disciples to relinquish their extra change of clothes in order to follow him, my reality made me uncomfortable. He didn't support them rotating two tunics, much less a lineup of quirky, seasonal wall art.

I felt the burn. Our faith does not require that we fit a tithe into our monthly budgets, schedule automatic payments to our church, and eventually forget cash is even changing hands.

What our faith inspires is the sort of foolish generosity that lives as though we believe we cannot outspend God. Our generosity can never outpace his. As painful as it initially was for me to read his words with a heart and two eyes that refused to look away, he does not tell us to keep what we need and share the rest.

Instead, he says to give all that we have, hoard nothing, and let him handle the bookkeeping.

If I say I follow him, I should care about the things he cares about. Even and especially if it costs me something. But it's one thing to understand and a whole 'nother thing to try to rewire a heart built on believing what's mine is mine.

● ▪ ●

You don't know how badly I wish I could tell you this generosity business comes easily to me. Back when I believed I was exceptionally generous, my frame of reference was built on the fact that I sometimes put cash bills into the Salvation Army bucket rather than loose pocket change. Still, at that time in our life, forking money over simply wasn't asking too much. We rarely even missed it.

I gave so I would keep getting. I had never practiced true generosity in lack. When I read the story of the rich, young ruler with my new eyes, I recognized myself. My face fell with his, because I, too, had many possessions, and the more we have, the more concerned we are with keeping it.

I wrote in chapter 3 about the ways God commandeered our finances, knocking the hardest decisions off our plate in gestures of profound grace. Just as he was showing us that we'd never even tasted real generosity, he reclaimed half of our income by rescuing me from my job, then doubled back and rescued Cory from his. His timing felt—how shall I say?—squirrelly.

In the very next breath, he tossed us into a new community, pummeled our hearts for his people, and threw ordinary, bare-cupboards need around us like fistfuls of glitter. On every side were people whose lack made our new state of "less" look like a fattened calf. There were neighbors who needed toilet paper and space heaters, friends in jail who needed socks and someone to talk to on the phone. There was a couple we barely knew who would be sent back to jail if they couldn't come up with fifty dollars to pay for their court-ordered anger management classes, and a young mom trying to make it back to her children states away.

It's tricky to talk about moving to an underresourced neighborhood. Inevitably, some well-meaning person will refer to my friends and neighbors as "the least of these."

Confession: I have always secretly struggled with referring to anyone as "the least of these." *I'm sorry, Jesus. It bugs me.* No matter who says it or how "relevant" that person is, it sounds kind of uppity. I don't care for the us-them ring to it. It feels a bit caste-system–ish.

God's people are abuzz right now about extending generosity to "the least of these." (Update: I don't even like to type it.) It's definitely progress. The problem is, if I'm referring to someone as "the least," what does that make me? The much better? The slightly holier? The fancier? The cleaner? The luckier? What?

Of course, Jesus did refer to some of his favorite people as "the least."

"I tell you the truth, when you did it to one of the least of these my brothers and sisters, you were doing it to me!" (Matt. 25:40).

Still, I can't shake the feeling that I am the official least, even if no one else can see it. Even if they refuse to believe me.

I know who I am, and I've seen what I'm capable of. Positioned against a blameless Savior who dispensed lavish proclamations of love and shocking truths about the grave conditions of a proud heart, yes, I am the very worst.

The longer we percolated in our new surroundings, finding ourselves positioned painfully near a good bit of heartache, the more it became imperative for us to come to a place of clarity about what the gospel required of us.

Crazy John was ready with another punch in the gut:

> If someone has enough money to live well and sees a brother or sister in need but shows no compassion—how can God's love be in that person? Dear children, let's not merely say that we love each other, let us show the truth by our actions. (1 John 3:17–18)

Where we used to talk about account balances and the trajectory of the stock market, Cory and I now found ourselves knee-deep in navigating a brand-new kind of financial conversation. How do we learn to traverse these waters? What does compassion look like? Are some needs worthy and others not? We can't say yes to everyone, can we?

I have an acquaintance who set her personal standard at saying yes to every request, automatically. She says it takes the pressure off to not have to make that decision, funneling real people with real needs into separate columns where one is deemed deserving and the other not. There's a big part of me that warms to this approach. It *would* simplify things. At the same time there are situations where we know that God has different plans.

Here's what we're learning more than anything else when it comes to bearing a generous heart, soft toward the need around us: giving is almost universally more about the condition of our hearts and what God has to show us than it is about the person at the receiving end. God cares just as much about my surrender as their need.

There are times we find ourselves wrestling about the "right" thing, but just as often, what we're really worried about is handing over what we think we deserve to keep. We all need to be rescued, just in different ways. As Robert D. Lupton, founder of Focused Community Strategies in Atlanta, wrote:

> [Jesus] chooses to show us his kingdom by personally feeding a hungry multitude rather than examining their motives or teaching them budgeting. He heals sick men and women and children without instructing them in preventive medicine.
>
> Why is this? Perhaps he knows the tendency of his followers to use our knowledge, our cause and effect theories, to pronounce judgment upon the suffering ones instead of healing them. He may know that we would prefer to create a program of service or champion a cause for the needy instead of risking the contagion of personal involvement. But he does not allow us to withdraw to the theoretical or theological. He forces us to feed, to clothe, to give a cup of water . . . His words and his life push us to the very place that will change us and fit us for his kingdom.[2]

I might have already mentioned that I'm a notorious slacker when it comes to praying. I'm sort of a flash-mob prayer, spontaneous, fleeting, and often desperate. I'm not of the DNA that commits every little decision to prayer. The Holy Spirit was sent to inhabit us from a place of deeply personal communion. His is the voice ever in our ear. Sometimes, when I stop to "ask," I am actually just stalling on what he's already shown me to be right.

There's certainly a place for discerning the Spirit when it comes to stewarding our finances. We should always avoid making a bad situation somehow worse, and we've faced situations where saying yes would have done exactly that. We've come to see that not every emergency should become *our* emergency. But as we continue to grasp how undeserving we are of the daily and eternal grace we receive, we're slower to deem someone else as undeserving of what we stand to offer.

My friend Heather, a former missionary to Haiti and one of the women God used in massive ways to disciple my faith in our early phases of free fall, reminded me more than once of the liberty found in walking toward those things with which God does not find fault. God does not find fault with a sharing heart, and operating under this mind-set inspires action.

I simply cannot foresee a circumstance where God will face us one day and say, "You know, I just wish you'd have kept more of your money for yourselves." It plainly does not align with the lay-it-down, let-it-go gospel that guides us.

I'm surprised to discover I want to be a "yes" person. I want to be the good news.

The best news I know is Jesus, and the way he insists on fussing around with us. He could do his thing while we do ours. He could do whatever he pleases. Shockingly, what pleases him is to bring us off the bench and into his game.

Cohosting the Feast

Food appears to be a fairly big deal to God and Jesus, and as a full-on foodie, I find it so endearing. Part of the grand design for Jesus' time on earth included clocking plenty of hours around the dinner table. Were it not for food, he wouldn't have had the pleasure of raising eyebrows when he ate with "scum" and schooling religious men when they balked about him keeping company with the wrong kinds of people.

Early in his ministry food took center stage when massive crowds gathered to hear him speak, then stayed for the entire day. Basically, a hostess's worst nightmare. It happened twice in Scripture, in close succession. First, the crowd of five thousand (Mark 6:35–44), followed by a crowd of four thousand (Mark 8:1–10).

Both scenarios unfolded almost identically. The crowd was famished. Jesus felt compassion for them. The disciples wigged.

They scramble around, worried and embarrassed, turning to Jesus, as if to say, "You got us into this mess . . ."

In both Matthew and Mark, just a few chapters apart, he answers with these words:

"How much bread do you have?"

He wasn't tied up or tired of helping. It wasn't one of those times where we imagine God being too busy, off solving bigger problems while our humdrum woes fall off the heavenly grid. Jesus wasn't trying to be funny or make his disciples feel stupid.

He was inviting them into his story, the same one that would redeem humanity.

Remember, Jesus was God's presence wrapped in skin. He

could have turned every stone at their feet into a cranberry scone. He could have walked Chilean bass straight out of the Sea of Galilee. He could have done something so shocking. *Poof!* Chips and salsa and tacos for all!

The problem was hunger, and there was no limit to the ways he could have solved it. He didn't need anyone's sad leftovers.

The disciples had just a little bit of bread, barely enough even for themselves. But Jesus gave them the option to fork it over, and when they did, God took their small, humble portion and stretched it across thousands of hungry people, with basketfuls left uneaten. He does the same for us.

That is who God is and how he loves us.

He invites us into smallness and less, so that when he swoops in and steals the show, when we see for ourselves that there is always plenty in his economy of abundance, when we take seriously our bit role in the rescue of his people, all the glory belongs to him.

Surveying the sum of creation, God looks at you and me and decides we're worthy allies. Each day brings a question: "How much bread do you have?"

If we dare to hand it over, it's multiplied.

Tonya

Last fall, I was on my way to get groceries (a chore of the privileged) and noticed my gas tank was well past "E."

I thought about filling up first, but my thrifty, save-a-buck instincts kicked in and I remembered the wondrous system of accruing fuel points based on my grocery receipt total.

Thirty minutes later, my van packed with a hundred bucks' worth of chicken thighs, tortillas, Earl Grey tea, cold cereal, and the like, I drove across the parking lot to fuel up.

Not two gallons in, a lady in an old beater pulled up beside me. I caught the distinct vibe that she wanted to talk to me, which could only mean she wanted something.

Every single time this happens, without exception, my instinct is to drop my gaze, get uber-serious about whatever I happen to be doing, and pretend I don't notice. I always want to hide. I hate myself for being the sort of woman who gets approached, feeling profiled in reverse. *I must look like the biggest sucker in the world.*

Reluctantly I walked over to her car, only because I couldn't avoid it.

She stopped dead in her tracks and screamed, "Are you a news reporter????!!!"

It wasn't quite what I was expecting. She followed it with, "And I'm not just saying that because I need your help!"

She needed money for gas, "a full tank if possible." In a testament to all I've learned along the journey from self and into freewheeling, surrendered community, I lied and told her all I had was ten dollars. Seriously, that marks progress in my life. I used to say I didn't have anything, and that was only if I was feeling generous enough to respond at all.

Whatever. I could spring for ten dollars' worth of gas for this woman. It wouldn't break me, and it might even make me feel good. But I wasn't filling her tank. That's just ridiculous.

All gutsy, she shot back with, "Well, you can use your credit card, then."

Who was this person? Why me? Then, like an arrow through

my puffed-up, gimme-gimme soul, I thought, *Well, yes. I suppose I can.*

In bearing witness to her need, my soul recognized her soul. This is the way of community, where we all have something to offer and we all have something we lack. He speaks our name in the beats between us, seeing a need and deciding it matters.

We chatted at the pump as I swiped my card. Her name was Tonya. Peeking into my van, she spotted Calvin's Bible. "You know God? I used to, but not anymore." She scratched her head, looked absentmindedly at the sky arching overhead. "I done so many sins."

"Girl, me too." *You have no idea, Tonya. You think you know, but you've got it all wrong.*

Hers is a long, unresolved riff of poverty and abuse. I heard as much as she could cram into a twelve-gallon space. I soaked it up, praying as the numbers spun on the pump that the right words would fall on her listening heart.

He already loves you, Tonya. Right this second. You don't have to change a thing. You never have to hide. He adores you. Run from that abuse, and don't look back. Run toward the promise buried under the wreckage of your pain. Just say his name. Search the sky for his hand. He's right there, and he loves you right now, in your mess. He is for you, and you can't be good on your own.

Every word from my lips doubled back and landed lightly in my own heart.

She was heading back to her home, a state away. A ripple of panic washed over me. This stranger, who found me in my need, wouldn't cross my path again. The truth landed like a dull punch of loss. Standing there, funneling my more into her less, I had met the bold, sincere face of Jesus, who will do what it takes to make me see his presence shimmering low in the shadows.

She kissed my cheek twice before driving away. She looked me square in the eye and said she loved me. I was her new little sister, and she would pray for me.

Tonya should be all the proof I need that God didn't structure this world as a badly bent system of Haves and Have Nots. I was never meant to save a soul, and no one was purposed as a project. We were meant to be comrades, mutually passing around whatever we have to offer.

If I believe my less ensures someone else's more, what else could I possibly need to know? Why is this dilemma so often a source of nagging conflict and emotional bartering instead of a simple no-brainer?

Will I ever come to the place of skipping the monkeying-around middle, where I pretend not to know what I definitely know for sure?

God is gentle sometimes, but he'll bring the fire if he has to. He'll burn the sky, drain the oceans, and knock us to our knees if that's what it takes to satisfy the need of his children. The need might be a tank of gas or the core ache to recognize our place in his family. Either way, the only fix is to step into our smallness and let him be great.

There is no such thing as Haves and Have Nots within God's upside-down community. We're all selling ourselves on the corner without grace. We're all split and bleeding without love. We're stronger together. We win because we're not alone.

We're all the Haves, set apart in purpose, placed in the light of community, taking chances every day, carrying the burdens of another because we're able, loving not out of obligation but desire, stubbornly believing in the face of all we see that we were made for this truth.

Watches over Wallets

Here's the bad news: generosity doesn't begin or end with wrecking our Dave Ramsey budgets and reaching into our cute, handmade bags. When it comes to a heart that meets the pulse of Christ's, all our resources are on the table. He doesn't just want anything; he wants everything.

Generosity is a condition of the heart, not the wallet. I know this, in part, because I'm surrounded by generous friends. There have been innumerable times where, with a simple gesture, my heart has been known; my worry or loneliness has met its end.

Between selling our farm and moving to the city, we rented a home that boasted, among other things, a carpeted kitchen and persnickety plumbing. These were gray days, and not only because I was trying my dangdest to potty-train Silas while beating back complicated feelings of loss and unrest. When my friend Kristin showed up with a pint of just-picked blueberries, I fell face-first onto my unmade bed and wept.

A few months later, in our first weeks in the new neighborhood, when I believed my only friend was the incessant train that kept me up all night, another friend knocked on my door with a jelly jar of zinnias and farm-grown raspberries. (A memo to the world: fruit is clearly my love language!)

The week Robert moved in, I received a care package with a card that read, "For the New Mom!" and I sobbed so hard I choked.

I could go on and on about the ministry of doughnuts and offers to babysit. In the past year alone I've been the recipient of countless "little" gifts and handwritten notes arriving just in the nick of time. They have always made a difference to me, costing the giver little more than her time and trouble.

Generosity is equal parts seeing and believing. I recognize your heartache, and I believe it can be healed. You would think with all these good examples surrounding me, I would more swiftly transfer what they teach me to my neighbors.

Honest to goodness, as hard as it can be to shelve my common sense and share my cash, it's so much harder to loosen my grip on my time.

I frequently field calls that open with, "Are you busy?" It always bugs the human, "I Am Important" part of me. *Uh, yes. I'm busy.* My work is elusive. I get it. My own kids are only vaguely aware of what I do while they're in school each day.

I'm totally doing things, okay? I have a schedule (of sorts). The question is, am I willing to hold my agenda with an open hand, ready for the Holy Spirit to charge in and take it? Does my life leave room for the unexpected?

On its own, no. I'm quite fond of the expected, and our culture tells me this is right. We praise time management and routine. We prize "me time" and "family time," and though there is absolutely a place for all of this, God operates well past the edges of our finite boundaries of today and this year and the "Wow, it's a busy month" we volley back and forth.

A couple of weeks ago I sat working on the manuscript for this book, buried inside my own head, tapping the keys, when my phone rang. "What are you doing today?"

"Well, I'm working . . ." It's hard to convey tone here, but let's just say I could probably stand to soften my edges a bit when these interruptions occur.

On the other end of that line, a gift waited just for me. It looked like an unscheduled hour spent driving one of my favorite neighbors to school after she'd missed the bus. Those thirty minutes with her in my passenger seat ended up being lovely. After weeks of hit-and-miss encounters, we had a chance to really connect. She opened up about hard things she was going through—the kinds of things that would send you or me straight to therapy. The drive was long enough that we had time to lighten up and laugh.

I reminded her that we are always her family. Forever. We'll never leave, like the others. We won't give up on her, and she can't use up her chances with us. These were things that needed to be said. She needed to hear them, and I needed to feel their weight against my lips.

We keep relearning that generosity might mean impossible amounts of time driving people around town—no license, no wheels, no insurance, or all of the above. We are invited to loosen the reins on our plans and give away some of our most prized resources. It's not so complicated after all to live out a ministry of saying hello. Maybe the biggest sacrifice we have to offer is a willingness to really listen and expect to learn.

In these small motions, extended not because we feel sorry or guilty, not because we're trying to earn something that was never for sale, we grow the most. She is me. They're us. We're them.

They need something that we have, and we're starting to care. That is only God. Only, ever God. He's dismantling our big ideas, and we're finding him there in the dust.

He offers the opportunity to experience a richness we'd never know if we remained locked in the prison of our false security and maximized agendas.

Here, in our everyday, he invites us in to the abundant life.

Holding Hands with the Tension

The struggle between stewarding our resources well and becoming more generous people is real. God can come along and strip away some of our excess, but we're still left with the everyday question of what it looks like to live in such a way that we aren't defaulting to "me first" at every single flipping turn.

On this side of our upending, it's easy to see how having less has allowed us to give more. Our smaller home, with its smaller mortgage, allowed Cory to accept the position as full-time chaplain of the jail, where his salary is cobbled together each year by churches across the county. Vocation impacts our lives in significant ways, and our lower overhead created the wiggle room to choose a career path that didn't depend on making a certain income.

Additionally, moving alongside struggling people has shifted our perspective from keeping up to letting go. Our giving is more intentional now. We enjoy partnering with people doing good kingdom work. On our best days, we see our resources almost as living things, able to do things other than lounge around and get fat. Dollar for dollar, it's possible we're actually giving less than when we were earning more, but our current circumstances continue to push us to a like-it-or-not place of greater sacrifice. Though this doesn't always feel super awesome, I have to believe it carries a few soul perks.

Unfortunately we're still just regular *us* living regular lives. We still have choices to make every day. What matters most? What are the conditions and limitations of my surrender? Predictably, as we attempt to negotiate our humanity with our calling, I teeter. I wobble right, then veer left. There is no fulcrum on these scales, no matter how desperate I am for a steady middle ground. Trust me, I've searched.

I'm starting to see that God prefers me living in this tension, where with every meaningless purchase, the reel of faces spins—faces of dear friends, our people whom we love, brothers and sisters a world away whom we've never met but who still live inside our hearts somehow.

I'm forced to let the Holy Spirit guide me, and I'm forced to accept and own my inevitable failures. I'm not naïve anymore. At least not with this one thing. I can't chalk my selfishness up to ignorance like I used to.

God doesn't change, but I've never heard the same about Satan. He seems to shift and wiggle into various holographic forms depending on where I am and how I'm struggling. You want to know what the devil looks like today? The Garnet Hill catalog, which magically began reappearing again two years after I'd canceled it, with its cushy, whimsical sheet sets and fifty-dollar throw-pillow covers.

There are days when I cave in peace, knowing I wasn't called to sainthood or even to the blessed sisterhood. Sometimes I'm invited to stand at the stony bank as grace rushes by, a river of wine. Excessive, maybe. Certainly more than what I needed.

There are other days when I do the exact wrong thing, and I know it. I take what wasn't mine. I default to pinning my identity down where moths will feast.

Truth is, I'm still Shannan, the girl who likes fashion and decorating, the girl with the rebellious streak, the girl whose heart has been stretched by the tension around me. I'm still me, the occasional if slightly-more-reluctant lapdog of this consumerist machine. Sometimes I walk away; sometimes I run rabid toward the mall.

The difference is, I never run alone now.

God created us for his glory, then concocted a plan to bring his kingdom down to earth through the work of his spirit and wonky you and me. He tells us we are brothers and sisters, and that our love for him will manifest itself through the ways we extend care and compassion to one another.

If we see one of our siblings in need, we will be driven to urgent compassion. Not a single day goes by where I don't see the need of a brother or sister, and I know the same is true for you. We have to jump in, but we've been warned since we buckled patent leather shoes onto our tiny Sunday feet not to be "of" this world we're in.

What on earth does that even mean?

It means our identity does not belong here, and we should live accordingly—quick to peel away from the world's wisdom and walk the small and unpopular way of truth. It means we will prioritize people over things and others over ourselves. It means we understand the kinship of eternity, and we will not turn away from a brother in need. We will not allow ourselves to become numb to the horror we see daily on our iPhones or in the people across the alley whose lives have been beaten down by a culture that does not make room for them. The world we're in might choose to disengage and circle in, but we are not of that mindset. We will walk toward the pain of another.

We know God can fix our middle-class problems. We thank him mindlessly for our lunch, veering off script just enough to remember a roof over our heads on rainy days. We pray for our sick aunt and the babies in Africa. We say we trust him. *We say we trust him.*

But all across our towns, other prayers fall hot and soak the pillow. Our brothers and sisters believe there's something bigger than themselves, but wonder if they've used up all their chances.

They beg for help, and Jesus looks at you and me and asks, "How much bread do you have?"

I'd have liked to see the water turn to wine or watch Lazarus rise up from his tomb. I missed those miracles. But if I dare to keep my eyes fully open, I'm given a front-row seat to God's epic show, where much and little, great and low are stirred together to accomplish his purpose for his kids.

Practicing generosity binds me closely with friends living poor and oppressed, often at the boot-end of justice. It reminds me of my own poverty, where in the light of eternity, we are all the least.

We can choose this unpopular path of brutally honest togetherness, not because we want to fix or win over our neighbor, not because we want to feel like a hero, but because we believe that when God called us all *his*, it made us a family.

As our circle widens, our grip loosens. Just ask Robert.

A FINAL NOTE ON FREEDOM

Quite simply, our deep gratitude to Jesus Christ is manifested neither in being chaste, honest, sober and respectable, nor in church-going, Bible-toting and Psalm-singing, but in our deep and delicate respect for one another.

—*THE RAGAMUFFIN GOSPEL*, BRENNAN MANNING[1]

SINCE I'M YOU and you're me and we're all basically the same person wrapped in different paper, I'm sure some of the words on these pages are making your heart beat faster. I know this, because I've been where you are and, in many ways, still stand right next to you, anxious to imagine what on earth might wait for me just past my line of sight.

I'm no expert, but our haphazard ride has taught me a couple of things so far: (1) Dreaming big often means dreaming small. (2) The only thing I have to offer, in all the land, is Christ. Often, the best way to share that gift is by offering more of flailing, falling-down *me*.

If you're wondering where to start, I can only say that for me, it began with the thought that there might be more to life than I assumed, followed by a prayer to begin seeing the world as God does. My prayer wasn't answered through a flashy burning bush or an angel appearing in my kitchen, but with a quiet nudge to simply start paying attention.

● ■ ◍

I once took a reading test in the seventh grade (reading teacher: Miss Reed!) that ended with this extra credit question: List a word with six syllables.

Six? Some of us gave up; others nearly inverted our brains trying. A few of us desperately searched the floorboards, the ceiling, and everything in between while rhythmically counting the syllables of everything we saw.

Hidden in plain sight, on a bottom shelf, was a box with the word *Encyclopedia* stamped across its side.

Miss Reed wasn't interested in who knew what. She was curious to know who was willing to take the time to observe our surroundings.

If we want to be better students of Jesus, loving like he does, we have to get better at noticing.

There's much to learn, and just like my recent failed attempt at watercolor painting, it starts with a good, long stare-session, coming nose to nose with the reality in front of us, whether it's a pitcher of wildflowers, a single mom at church, or the tired side of town.

If you don't know where to start, just look around the room. Poke around the lowest shelves.

One friendship leads to another, and over time, like my paint-soaked brush swirled through a jar of water, some of those friendships fade and bleed into something luminous and new. We each leave our me-shaped mark, and the water turns blue, then green.

We become a family, in all its hodgepodge finest.

I would have never had the wisdom, guts, or patience to choose this life for myself. I thought what I wanted was the path of least resistance. But God knew what I was made for—what I truly wanted—and graciously showed me, inch by inch, that I could trust him with my future, my hours, my debit card, and my kids.

We're alive and blooming, sometimes "angsting," right here in the land of the living, where God's presence trips us up in the crumbling sidewalks and falls around us through the wispy curls of cigarette smoke. He won't waste a moment of pain, and he alone holds the power to stretch the soup into something even more savory.

He'll do the same for you.

Just last month a compassionate dentist told Silas, "It's okay that you're nervous. That way when you're all done, you can say, 'I was brave!'"

It made me tear up, the way she spoke truth into my little guy.

We all know that feeling. Falling into the will of God takes guts and grit we don't have. Of course we're nervous. *We can't handle this alone.*

And that's precisely the point.

Let's not let fear stop us from being the good news to a world desperate to be known by God's love. There's work to be done, and we were handpicked for the team, but if we want to see his goodness, we've got to drop our torn-up nets and follow him even as the bile rises in our throats and people snicker.

Get a good look at the cliff in front of you, the one you find yourself inching away from, the one you try to deny. Step close enough to peek over the edge and see just how far the fall might be. With any measure of luck, you might begin to see the beauty of the fall.

We get to collaborate with greatness. We're offered the freedom of seeing the way God is impossibly smitten with us. But first, we've got to be willing to fall.

We identify with the beggar and find more of him.

We discover our kinship with the criminal, the forgotten, the piercingly ordinary, and he is there.

The pulse of our humanity means we'll never get it right, and we weren't meant to.

God's love for us is a wheel that keeps turning, a cycle of capture and release. He gives and takes; we receive and pass it on. We are so much better together here, in this long-strung tension between what we think we deserve and the wild grace we've been given.

This is who God is. This is how he loves us.

ACKNOWLEDGMENTS

WRITING *FALLING FREE* has been a lot like living the life that inspired it—slow and warp-speed, delightful and angsty. Over the uneven terrain, I'm grateful to have had so many hands holding me (mostly) steady.

Cory, the world beyond our walls might never understand all you endured to make this happen. But I do. You have a gift for seeing people not as they are in a single moment, but for who they are constantly becoming. I'm the most grateful recipient of that grace. I love you like asphalt and peonies, pastures and graffiti.

Robert, Calvin, Ruby, and Silas, thanks for being quiet when you wanted to be crazy and for making me see that, sometimes, crazy is best. I love you like salsa and spring, and then some.

Mom and Dad, you put me on a plane to Belgium for a month when I was eleven. As the mom of an eleven-year-old now, I can only hope I'd have the guts to do the same. I'm forever grateful for the ways you inspired adventure and for the fearlessness with which you let me test my wings. No one else could have better prepared me for the thrill of free-fall.

Sarah, Kim, Timi, and Megan, thank you for diving into the weeds with me over chocolate croissants, fancy pizzas, and gone-cold tea. I want to grow old returning the favor.

Emily, you told me years ago to stop hem-hawing around and admit I was a writer. Thank you for the generous hours of reflecting, for asking the best questions, and for answering the silliest ones with a straight face.

Jen, my partner in brine, I found you just in the nick of time and was left with no choice but to strong-arm you into an online friendship. You continue to help me make sense of both the everyday and the eternal. I will never stop sending you pickles.

Jeane, you're an enthusiastic cheerleader in Converse tennies. Thank you for believing in me when this felt like a pipe-dream and for pushing me to do the work.

My (in)courage sisters, I am the glad benefactor to your drawing a wider circle and so grateful to learn from you and with you.

Jessica Wong, I didn't know to hope for an editor who would begin asking for updates on my friends and neighbors, but I got it with you. Thank you for making this book the best it could be and for answering my most tiresome questions with the patience of a saint.

To the entire team at Nelson, particularly Stephanie, Janene, and Sara, thank you for walking with me and enthusiastically believing in this book.

Andrew Wolgemuth, my agent, you have tirelessly championed my work and provided timely doses of calming and humor. I thank my lucky stars for you.

Mr. Miles, Dr. Spivey, Dr. Young, and Robert Rector, you planted tiny seeds of belief that perhaps I had a knack for writing.

Though I took the long way to the conclusion, I remember your kind words often.

David Platt, through the Holy Spirit alive in you, my family's life was changed forever. Thank you for telling hard truths and for sketching the bones of our new normal.

Nichole Nordeman, you wrote the soundtrack for my life and I'll never stop singing along.

The Electric Brew, thank you for the hot Earl Grey, the white noise, the community, and the space. Every time I Instagram a photo of you, the crowd goes wild. You're just that cool.

To my blog readers, I'm profoundly incapable of articulating what your support and friendship have meant to me over the past eight years. On one of my hardest days, you baked loaf after loaf of warm, virtual banana bread and I've never felt more sustained by imaginary food. I love you forever. In so many ways, this book is for you.

To my neighbors (and I'm stretching that word for all it's worth), you are among my favorite guides on this journey toward understanding God's goodness. Thank you for trusting me with your stories. I'm honored to live here with you in the land of the living.

NOTES

Chapter 1: Get Risky

1. David Platt, *Radical: Taking Back Your Faith from the American Dream* (Colorado Springs: Multnomah Books, 2010), 181.
2. www.themochaclub.org.
3. https://livefashionable.com.

Chapter 2: Redefine Family

1. Emily P. Freeman, *A Million Little Ways: Uncover the Art You Were Made to Live* (Grand Rapids, MI: Revell, 2013), 69.

Chapter 3: Have Less

1. Dietrich Bonhoeffer, *The Cost of Discipleship* (New York: Touchstone, 1995), 178.
2. *Merriam-Webster's 11th Collegiate Dictionary*, s.v. "freedom."

Chapter 4: Unplan

1. Deidra Riggs, *Every Little Thing: Making a World of Difference Right Where You Are* (Grand Rapids, MI: Baker Books, 2015), 107.

Chapter 5: Live Small

1. Emily P. Freeman, *Simply Tuesday: Small-Moment Living in a Fast-Moving World* (Grand Rapids, MI: Revell, 2015), 36.
2. Quoted in a personal meeting.
3. Gregory Boyle, *Tattoos on the Heart: The Power of Boundless Compassion* (New York: Free Press, 2010), 67.

Chapter 6: Gather

1. David Z. Nowell, *Dirty Faith: Bringing the Love of Christ to the Least of These* (Bloomington, MN: Bethany House, 2014), 44.
2. *thestanleyclan.com*.

Chapter 7: Open the Door

1. Louis Jaucourt, chevalier de, "Hospitality," *The Encyclopedia of Diderot & d'Alembert Collaborative Translation Project*, trans. Sophie Bourgault, http://quod.lib.umich.edu/d/did/did2222.0002.761/—hospitality?rgn =main;view=fulltext.
2. http://www.flowerpatchfarmgirl.com/2013/03/summoning-storm .html.
3. http://www.flowerpatchfarmgirl.com/2014/07/i-believe-in-tacos.html.

Chapter 8: Grow Together

1. Elyse M. Fitzpatrick and Jessica Thompson, *Give Them Grace: Dazzling Your Kids with the Love of Jesus* (Wheaton, IL: Crossway, 2011), 126.
2. Mark and Jan Foreman, *Never Say No: Raising Big-Picture Kids* (Colorado Springs: David C. Cook, 2015), 128.
3. Nicole Baker Fulgham, *Educating All God's Children: What Christians Can—and Should—Do to Improve Public Education for Low-Income Kids* (Grand Rapids, MI: Brazos Press, 2013), 20.

Chapter 9: Commune

1. C. Christopher Smith and John Pattison, *Slow Church: Cultivating Community in the Patient Way of Jesus* (Downers Grove, IL: IVP Books, 2014), 68.
2. "Come, Ye Sinners, Poor and Needy" by Joseph Hart, http://cyberhymnal .org/htm/c/o/m/comeyspn.htm.

Chapter 10: Give More

1. *Oxford Pocket Dictionary of Current English*, 2nd ed., s.v. "generous."
2. Robert D. Lupton, *Theirs Is the Kingdom: Celebrating the Gospel in Urban America* (New York: HarperCollins, 2010), 63.

A Final Note on Freedom

1. Brennan Manning, *The Ragamuffin Gospel: Good News for the Bedraggled, Beat-Up and Burnt Out* (Colorado Springs: Multnomah Books, 2015), 109.

ABOUT THE AUTHOR

SHANNAN MARTIN, KNOWN for her popular blog ShannanMartinWrites.com (formerly *Flower Patch Farmgirl*), is a speaker and writer who found her voice in the country and her story in the city. She and her jail-chaplain husband, Cory, have four funny children who came to them across oceans and rivers. Having sold their dream farmhouse, they now enjoy neighborhood life in Goshen, Indiana.